THE
DISRUPTED
EXECUTIVE

How to Move from a
Permanent Executive to a
Portfolio Way of Working

PAT LYNES

Rethink

First published in Great Britain in 2023
by Rethink Press (www.rethinkpress.com)

Cover image © Shutterstock | MJgraphics

This book is dedicated to my father, Diarmuid Lynes, who has been a significant influence on my career and continues to be sharp as a razor at 73, leading a portfolio lifestyle and acting as chairman of my business Sullivan & Stanley.

Contents

Foreword

Had you been born in the past, what might you have done for work? Assuming you are intelligent, hardworking and good with people, you could have risen to an important status in society and seized the best opportunity of the day.

Had you been alive in feudal times, you could have been a knight, commanding the ranks of the armed forces. In the agricultural age, perhaps you would have worked closely with the landed gentry to expand their realms. In the Mercantilist era, you might have commanded a fleet of trade ships. In the Industrial Revolution, you could have set up a factory and produced important goods.

What about now? What is the best opportunity for someone like you in today's economy? Have things changed in recent years and how should you respond?

The Disrupted Executive looks at the importance of aligning yourself with the best opportunities in the time in which you live. It also looks at the importance of adjusting the way you work when circumstances change. There's no point being the CEO of Blockbuster when digital movies are taking over.

Times have changed. Digital technology was transforming industries throughout the 2010s but in the 2020s it has gathered pace and the way we live and work has moved permanently onto a new axis. Office buildings are still empty and workers have radical new expectations about the way they should work. Talent is moving around at speed and big companies are adapting as fast as they can.

The industrial revolution working model is crumbling. Employers don't want to build large, loyal workforces any more and talent doesn't trust that loyal, long-term engagement is the key to prosperity. This isn't to say that companies don't need talent and talent doesn't want to perform. It's just that the nature of the win-win relationship is being redefined.

In the years ahead, the pace of disruption will accelerate. The generative AI genie is out of the bottle and expanding rapidly across every working environment.

Originally experts thought artificial intelligence would disrupt low-skilled jobs and 'higher-ups' would be completely unaffected. At first glance, it would appear the opposite is true. AI has swept in to disrupt knowledge working, decision-making, governance, compliance and many of the things executive teams do.

In the first few months of ChatGPT going live, over 100 million people started using AI. It has been the fastest adoption of technology in history. If we thought digital technology had already shaken things up, it turns out that the biggest changes are yet to come.

As a result, you have the opportunity to shape your career in a way that aligns with your goals as well as the extraordinary times we are in. Over the past ten years, I have watched as Pat Lynes built a successful international business to capitalise on the future of work. Sullivan & Stanley has become the go-to consultancy for big brands that want to create positive and lasting change. Pat has had a front row seat in watching thousands of executives and leaders transform their workplaces. He's also witnessed first-hand the career progression of some of the world's most sought-after talent.

Pat has observed that the most dynamic and in-demand leaders aren't chasing the safe, well-worn path. They are skewing towards a new executive path that is being defined by frontier change-makers, in real time. This book shares with you the insights and predictions that Pat has developed after working with some of the world's most valued executives as they navigate life on their terms.

There's never been a more important time to embrace being a disrupted executive and building a life and a career that you love.

Daniel Priestley
Author of *Entrepreneur Revolution* and founder of Dent Global

Introduction

I founded Sullivan & Stanley in 2016 to pioneer and champion new ways of working for both individuals and organisations. We are now an award-winning consultancy disruptor that deploys expert teams from our network, The Change Society, to solve the challenges companies face when undertaking change.

My background is in interim recruitment, and before founding Sullivan & Stanley I spent over twenty years working in senior roles in recruitment, first for Harvey Nash, where I built a division from scratch and turned it into a seven-figure revenue business, and then at La Fosse Associates, which I scaled to a healthy nine-figure revenue business in just over six years, winning many awards along the way.

Interim management has always been my game, and my father brought me up to take a community-first approach to things. I enjoy building communities of experts and associate experts and getting to know those experts, and then connecting them to problems and opportunities at board level.

I've worked at the cutting edge of market sentiment in businesses and with executive leaders. This placed me in the fortunate position of being able to observe the changes that were happening within interim recruitment and consulting, and gave me insight into what the future of work could look like.

When I worked at La Fosse, each week I spoke to ten or more senior executives and went into three or four different businesses. Over a twenty-year period, that's a lot of conversations. I gained insight and I built relationships, which is what I enjoy doing the most. I've always been a headhunter, a community-builder and a specialist in interim management by trade, but I started to fall out of love with the older-style recruitment model. I could see that the world of work was changing, and I felt that I needed to refresh, reinvigorate and reinvent myself, but at the time I wasn't sure I had enough experience, or enough of a network, to be able to do something about it.

In the time that I was at Harvey Nash and La Fosse, I saw big programmes failing, big transformations failing and people failing to achieve their ambitions but still falling into the arms of big management consultancies expecting them to fix it. This is a false economy – on the whole, the management consultant model isn't designed to get you *out* of a problem. It's designed to keep you *in* the problem.

I saw that there was a fundamental change in the way that most people want to perform their work and realised there was a real opportunity for me to make a difference in the market. When organisations want to change and transform, they use either recruitment companies or management consultancies, and there's nothing in between.

With that backdrop, I saw the chance to create a business that challenged the traditional ways of recruiting and offered a new way of working for both individuals and businesses. My business, Sullivan & Stanley, was born out of a vision to inspire the future of work and to unite global experts. It provides consultancy and delivery services to corporates and fast-growth companies in a community-based way. Fundamentally, something had to change, and that's why Sullivan & Stanley exists.

My first book, *The Interim Revolution*,[1] advocates interim management and expounds the theory that interims are the most underused route to capability.

---

1   P Lynes, *The Interim Revolution: How crowdsourcing, the on-demand gig economy and teams as a service are transforming business globally* (Writing Matters Publishing, 2017)

I believe that the top 5% of all expertise and capability is in the independent knowledge worker sector, and I saw that trend exploding over the years. *The Interim Revolution* is an introduction to the knowledge gig economy and presents a new way for businesses to transform by harnessing the power of a team as a service approach to solve business problems and deliver successful outcomes.

In *The Disrupted Executive*, I build on the ideas presented in *The Interim Revolution* while introducing the concept of portfolio working as a way for senior executives to transform their lives and create their own world of work that is both fulfilling and exciting.

People love having independence, autonomy and the option to choose the work that they do, when they want to do it. When people realise that they're sitting on a gold mine of experiences and expertise and that they can monetise themselves, the result is both liberating and lifechanging.

I help coach people in how to do that. If you're out there building a network, talking to lots of people, exploring different interests, writing content and contributing to society, you're going to become a more well-rounded person with an appetite for personal growth.

Life's about having choices, and this book is written to help you understand the choices you have. You can take steps to futureproof yourself so you don't become disrupted should market conditions change. I'll show you how to make the jump from your permanent role into a new, sustainable and plural way of working which will give you work-life integration and results in a longer, more fulfilling and more rewarding life.

I'm constantly meeting senior executives who are struggling and burnt out because of the corporate system. They feel frustrated because they're trapped by financial commitments and are stressed out because they feel there's no way out and no other way to be. I've been there, and it's horrible.

If you're a senior executive, a senior leader or a senior knowledge worker in an SME or a corporate and you're feeling burnt out and ground down by the eighty-hour week and your twenty days of holiday a year and want to live differently, then this book is for you. There is a wealth of opportunities out there for you to capitalise on, and I can show you how.

You deserve to live a life that is balanced and fulfilling and in which you're operating as the best version of yourself. This book will serve as the bridge that will get you from where you are now to where you want to be in three to five years. You are your own pension, and you need to invest in yourself just as you invest in your finances. The world of work can be a great place, but you must take charge of your destiny. This decade could be the best decade you've ever seen, or it could be the worst. Which will you choose?

By creating a new way of working, and new ways of thinking about work, I hope to inspire my children, Sullivan and Stanley, to create a world of work that works for them. And I want to help you do the same.

1
The World Of Work Isn't Working

It's no secret that the world of work is rapidly changing. The established way of doing things is slowly but surely being ripped to pieces, and we all want to go to new and better places.

If you've realised that the corporate dream has failed, and you want to awaken an entrepreneurial spirit to work in a different, more authentic way, this book will be your guide. It will give you all the information and resources you need to make the jump from a permanent to a portfolio way of working, which will help you start living a more fulfilling life.

My dad introduced me to the world of business. He's been a huge influence in my life, and many of my business decisions have been based on his experiences. My dad was a retail banker and worked for the same company for over forty years, from the age of eighteen until he was fifty-eight. Like many of his contemporaries, he climbed the corporate ladder and worked his way up – in his case, from bank clerk to divisional CEO of a global Irish bank.

As a family, we moved around a lot as my dad pursued his career. He used to work every Sunday, and on holidays he was kind of there, but he also kind of wasn't. I'm not complaining – my dad's work gave us a lot of opportunities, and I had a great upbringing, but we didn't see an awful lot of him. My dad worked hard all his life and then, about fifteen years before he retired, he got an opportunity to become a board executive with his bank. He chose the equity and shares over doing the thing that he loved, which was being with his customers. He built up a lot of equity and earned a lot of money, but he wasn't really happy, and he fell out of love with his job. He was frustrated a lot of the time and was sometimes hard to be around.

Then, in 2008, about six months before he retired, the global credit crunch happened, and his shares went from 21 euros a share down to 12 cents. He lost everything he'd been working for, and he retired with a lot of regret about spending the last fifteen years doing something for money rather than purpose.

When dad retired, he went from a high-power corporate role to doing essentially nothing. He played golf, lunched and drove my mum mad, and he just wasn't the same. He lost his sense of purpose, and in the space of two years, he put on three stone and started going downhill physically. He was heartbroken.

Watching my dad do a job that he didn't like for fifteen years and get nothing from it really affected me, and I knew that there had to be a different way of working.

If you've reached a point in your life or career where you've started to question what you're doing and why you're doing it, perhaps it's time to open the door to a new way of working.

My journey into business

I grew up in North London, and on Saturdays my dad often took me to meet his clients before the Arsenal game. At the time, there was a vibrant Irish scene in North London, and the place had an exciting multicultural, cosmopolitan feel.

Before the match, my dad would take me to the local pizza shop and we'd meet Gio and his family. Dad would talk to Gio, and I'd be given free pizza and as much lemonade as I could drink. Dad would agree to give Gio the funding to expand his branches by three or four, and then we'd go to the local butcher, where a similar scene would unfold. This was how he did business, and it taught me a lot about serving the community and creating opportunities. The concept of connecting people with opportunities was something I grew up with.

My initial foray into business was in 1999 when I was at university. I promoted, and then monetised, a DJ community and created the first website for hard house, techno and trance. I built the platform with a friend and we got a lot of interest from DJs, promoters, record-label bosses and club owners. What started out as an online fan scene exploded and soon went viral around Europe. Suddenly, I was connecting people and creating opportunities on a global scale. From then on, I knew that this was what I wanted to be doing.

My first job after university was at Harvey Nash, a global IT recruitment company. Recruitment was a natural fit for me, and I continued connecting people with opportunities by building networking groups that enabled senior-level professionals to access opportunities within telecoms. As my career progressed, I became a division director and later a board director.

I then hit a point where I started questioning what I was doing, partly because of what had happened to my dad.

I'd built a company for someone else, and at first I loved it because I was dealing with customers, running a sales team and doing senior recruitment – all things I enjoyed doing. But I took the board position to operationally grow a business with increased equity and sold myself out. That's when I started hating the work.

I remember asking my dad, 'What do I do? I don't enjoy going to work, and I feel trapped because I'm being paid a six-figure salary and I've got 5% equity in this business. Why isn't it enough?'

What it boiled down to was this – I knew that if I went down the path of corporate executive, in five to ten years I'd probably be the most overpaid recruitment COO in the UK. I'd have no network, I'd have stopped learning and, if the sector changed, I'd be unemployable.

I realised that it was time to disrupt myself.

> 'Sometimes leaving all that you know, the routine, the process and the security, can be daunting. Rest assured, from someone that has done exactly that, what lies ahead is exciting – you get to define your rules, your culture and your values to take your business on the flightpath of your design. It's flying high at its very best!'
> — **Mandy Hickson, former jet pilot**

The fourth industrial revolution

It's clear that the old way of working isn't working anymore. Nothing is permanent, so the idea of having permanent staff should be challenged. I've seen organisations and executives go on big drives to recruit permanent leaders and staff. It takes ages because it's hard to get permanent staff and most organisations don't hire correctly. Many established organisations become wedded to a particular path, simply replacing those who have left rather than evaluating the roles that are right for the organisation.

In fact, even if organisations do hire permanent staff correctly, they probably don't host them correctly and end up losing them anyway. There's this ongoing process of hiring permanent people that's just not feasible. Organisations can hire great people, but then force them to fit into the wrong operational model, where they're managed on projects rather than outcomes.

The COVID-19 pandemic made this even more obvious, and seeing the way that the pandemic disrupted businesses was a catalyst for me to write this book. I wanted to help people navigate the new ways of working and encourage them to take the opportunities that they're now presented with.

We're at the beginning of the fourth industrial revolution. In the first industrial revolution, water and steam mechanised production; in the second, electric power created mass production; and in the third, electronics and information technology automated production. The fourth industrial revolution will take automation to a level which will blur the lines between physical, digital and human spheres and use technology to perform tasks previously carried out by humans.[2]

We're heading into a decade of absolute seismic transformation, not just for the business world but also the political world. Boundaries are changing and new technologies are being created all the time, and anything that can be automated will be. Some roles will be lost, and I estimate that by 2030, 50% of companies will be seeking to automate processes and considerably decrease their number of full-time staff.[3]

The days when you would leave school, get a job for life, work hard for your pension, and live for your weekends, holidays and (a brief) retirement are coming to an end.

---

2   K Schwab, 'The Fourth Industrial Revolution: What it means, how to respond', World Economic Forum, January 2016, www.weforum.org/agenda/2016/01/the-fourth-industrial-revolution-what-it-means-and-how-to-respond

3   'Machines will do more tasks than humans by 2025 but robot revolution will still create 58 million net new jobs in the next five years', World Economic Forum, 17 September 2018, www.weforum.org/press/2018/09/machines-will-do-more-tasks-than-humans-by-2025-but-robot-revolution-will-still-create-58-million-net-new-jobs-in-next-five-years

Research from Blue Zones (regions where people live longer) tells us that if you feel as if you're no longer a valued member of a tribe, if you haven't got a strong purpose, you can start to degenerate – because you've signalled to your body you're on the way out.[4] The adrenaline goes, the mitochondria start to die, the purpose dies. Your kids stick you in a home, you die. And that's just the way the Western world has always worked.

But it doesn't have to be like this.

The new way of working is flexible, fluid and outcome-based, not time-based. Progressive organisations will introduce operating models centred on attracting and engaging workers on projects according to a statement of works document. Once the works are complete, the workers will be released.

I don't believe in the concept of permanent work anymore. 'Permanent' means 'forever', and that's the old way of working. The old way is all about the ownership of talent, but forward-thinking businesses are starting to realise that it's not about *owning* talent but about having *access* to talent.

The common problem I find when I help organisations transform is that they've got legacy people on expensive permanent contracts. These people are too

---

4   D Buettner, 'Reverse engineering longevity', Blue Zones, no date, www.bluezones.com/2016/11/power-9

scared to move on, they don't realise what they don't know and they end up impeding the organisation.

It's time for knowledge workers and senior executives to start thinking about how they can make themselves vital, not functional, by building a business around their expertise. There are opportunities to ride the wave of massive transformation and capitalise on it while also living the life that you want.

WORKFORCE AGILITY

According to a PwC study, nearly half of HR professionals (46%) expect at least a fifth of their workforce to be contractors or temporary workers by 2022: 'In an age of disruption, innovation and transformation, opportunities have never been greater. But for organisations to take advantage of this, agility is essential.'[5]

Disrupt or die

For corporations, this decade is a time to disrupt and reinvent or die – and it's the same for individuals. You need to think about what's really keeping you in your job. The salary? The equity? What happens if your

---

5   PwC, 'Workforce agility', no date, www.pwc.co.uk/services/human-resource-services/human-resource-management/workforce-agility.html

role becomes obsolete and you've sat there for the best years of your life and have nothing to show for it?

All generations are looking for different ways of working, and if a business hasn't got purpose and people aren't being given a variety of work, employees are going to vote with their feet. We're seeing a shift away from an employee mentality to a value-provider mentality. People no longer want to feel like a dispensable cog in a machine.

The government isn't going to look after you any more. According to the Pensions Policy Institute, by the time we retire we can expect a few hundred pounds per week at best.[6] And on the whole, corporates don't really care about you. The world of work is changing at an accelerated pace, and the next generation isn't going to know, or care, who you are unless you move with the times and make yourself relevant.

The fourth industrial revolution will have as much impact on the world as the shift from horses to cars did, but this doesn't have to scare you. Running parallel to these changes in the workplace are increased opportunities to disrupt our careers and reinvent ourselves. We can access online training, travel more easily, work remotely and connect with people from all over the world through our laptops.

---

6   www.pensionspolicyinstitute.org.uk/media/kluac5mw/20230831-ppi-pension-facts.xlsx

Now is the time to disrupt, and it's also the best time in the world to do it.

Summary

- The world of work is changing rapidly. We're heading into a decade of massive transformation and a new way of working. The old way of working was about ownership of talent, the new is about having access to talent.

- Knowledge workers and senior executives must create a business around their expertise in order to become vital rather than merely functional.

- This is the time to self-disrupt and grab the opportunities ahead; open your eyes to a new way of working.

In the next chapter, I'll ask you to consider what the future of work might look like for you.

2
The Human Movement

The future of work is changing, and it's time to think about what that means for workers. We must consider what we need to do as individuals to ensure that the world of work continues to work for us.

The future of work

Based on the media, it would seem as if we're heading towards a somewhat-dystopian future where humans are slowly phased out. We know that more and more business processes are being automated and that artificial intelligence (AI) is becoming more prevalent within our everyday lives, and it's easy to feel despair.

But despite all the fearmongering, humans are very much at the heart of the future of work. When I think about my sons, Sullivan (aged eleven) and Stanley (aged nine), and their future, I'm excited about what technology will enable them to do in their working lives. Technology gives us all an opportunity to raise the game by outsourcing some more menial tasks and automating simplistic processes.

I think that in the future, technology will develop and enable humans to do what humans do best: be creative and innovative, create value and build meaningful relationships. Humanity and human-to-human interactions will be prioritised, and there will be a focus on emotional intelligence, collaboration and project-based work.

In fact, with the automation of the workspace, there will be *more* time to focus on the human-to-human interactions. With AI taking over the menial roles, there'll be more time for creative thinking and connecting with others on a human level.

It's time for the human movement.

'I have searched for many years across corporate, contract and consulting environments to understand what provides me with a greater feeling of fulfilment. Ultimately helping others to improve across a varied landscape is my sweet spot. The best environment is one that doesn't confine me and enables me to be more curious and have a growth mindset to embrace challenges, learn from mistakes and be inspired by great people.

Sadly few corporate environments do this well, in many cases the opposite. Simon Sinek talks about how the military rewards those that sacrifice themselves for others, whereas businesses tend to reward those who sacrifice others for themselves. The majority of the corporate workforce is promoted for what they are good at doing, not for making people around them better. Let's keep disrupting.'

— Mark Johnson, IT leader

I believe the future workplace will be much better than the current workplace – a human-to-human workplace based on respect, autonomy and diversity. Hierarchies will start to decentralise, as the pandemic has shown, and both individual workers and companies will seek out greater meaning and more relevance within society. We're moving towards a society which will value social interactions and community over commerce. This is an emerging theme in the United States. Socially responsible business models are starting to make their presence felt.[7]

---

7   M Gavin, '5 examples of corporate social responsibility that were successful', Harvard Business School Online, 6 June 2019, https://online.hbs.edu/blog/post/corporate-social-responsibility-examples

Graduates in all disciplines are beginning to realise that education isn't a direct passport to employment, and they're seeing job roles disappear overnight. Young people are fairly dissatisfied with what's on offer. It's not just young people, though. Workers in their thirties, forties and fifties are also seeing how quickly life can change and how the corporate dream is dying, and they want to have more control over their work and their lives.

Then there are the environmental factors. Huge corporations are destroying the environment, and people don't want to be associated with that any more. People are starting to see that there are better ways to work. They no longer want to work for faceless corporations that have no purpose other than to generate profit. They no longer want to sell out to the corporate dream. They want to feel that they're doing something worthwhile and contributing to something meaningful.

The world of work used to be about security – about having a job for life – but things are changing. Many want to live a more holistic life that enables them to achieve personal fulfilment. This is why we're starting to see a shift towards portfolio ways of working.

It's about recognising that people from different generations, even ones who believed they'd have just one or two jobs in their lives, now think it's unlikely they're going to spend an entire career in one industry, let alone one company.

Four generations in the workplace

The workplace has changed dramatically in the past decade. Now, there are four generations working alongside each other.

THE FOUR GENERATIONS[8]

Baby boomers: Born between 1946 and 1964, they're now between 57 and 75 years old. There are currently 14.8 million in the UK.

Generation X: Born between 1965 and 1980, they're now between 41 and 56 years old. There are currently 13 million in the UK.

Generation Y (Millennials): Born between 1981 and 1995, they're now between 26 and 40 years old. There are currently 13.4 million in the UK.

Generation Z: Born between 1996 and 2012, they're now between 9 and 25 years old. There are currently nearly 16 million in the UK.[9]

Generation Z workers in particular are looking to do work they feel is of value to society, make meaningful connections, get fluid gig work and have the opportunity to work from anywhere in the world in a way

---

8   R Waugh, 'The 5G workforce', Telegraph Spark, www.telegraph. co.uk/business/tips-for-the-future/workforce
9   D Clark, 'Population of the United Kingdom in 2020, by age', Statista, no date, www.statista.com/statistics/281174/uk-population-by-age

that suits them. Employers won't be able to attract this type of worker if they don't have a humane approach to their business operations.

I'm a Millennial, and my generation wants to put their energy and expertise into creating products and services that they can design a life around.

Generation X and the baby boomers are the ones leading the charge in portfolio working. They are the experts and want to work on multiple opportunities, rather than be tied to a job for life.

The businesses that understand that things are shifting and realise that a new operating model is required will be the ones that thrive in the future. Businesses will need to change their operating systems. If they can do this, they'll reap the reward of being able to access the best brains and skills from all around the world. The businesses that don't change things up are really going to suffer.

Why do people want something else?

There's no longer a limit to your working life. You're no longer 'over the hill' at fifty-five or sixty, and some people are becoming entrepreneurs in their seventies. In fact, my dad is a good example of this.

After spending a couple of years without any drive and feeling regret for having wasted a lot of his career working in a role that didn't suit him, my dad decided to go back to work – but in a way that *did* suit him. Now, he's checked himself into a portfolio way of working. He's the chairman of a housing association, he does ad-hoc consulting, sits on the board of the local church and now he's also chairman of my business. He's got a routine, he's keeping his brain sharp and he's got purpose – he's serving the church, the housing association and my business. In fact, he recently chaired the Sullivan & Stanley board meeting and called us out on things that we weren't even thinking about. That's pretty good for a seventy-three-year-old!

The point is that there's a lot of human capital out there. There's a lot of value and experience and potential which isn't being used because businesses are unwilling, or unable, to access it.

In the near future, portfolio working could be a core part of the expert economy. More and more people are becoming entrepreneurs because they don't want to dance to somebody else's tune. People don't want to live a life where they're tied to a single employer, or to a set way of doing things. There's a general dissatisfaction and a belief that there's a better way of living. This is where portfolio working comes in. Senior executives, senior knowledge workers and people at the top of their game are seeing that life is too short to be pigeonholed into a career that bores them.

Avoiding the retirement trap

With the future of work changing, one of the most important things you can do for yourself is avoid the whole notion of retirement. Being retired mean you're no longer growing, no longer useful – simply getting ready to die. It's a flawed concept.

The concept of retirement was created in the nineteenth century, and it was based on the fear of Marxism. German chancellor Otto von Bismarck realised that those most likely to become Marxist revolutionaries were young, unemployed men, so his government created a system called retirement to get the older people out of the marketplace to make room for the younger men.[10] Retirement is an old concept that isn't relevant in the same way today – and it's not relevant at all for entrepreneurs.

Many people stop learning, stop developing ideas, stop building relationships and stop meeting new people when they retire. Retiring at a certain age is seen as normal in society, but you don't need to

---

10 N Pasricha, 'Why retirement is a flawed concept', *Harvard Business Review*, 13 April 2016, https://hbr.org/2016/04/why-retirement-is-a-flawed-concept

remain stuck in this mindset. Don't talk yourself into being taken out of use, and don't think yourself into an early grave.

Outside-in: raising the profile of key talent

Employers who want to attract top talent will need to adjust to a workforce that's geared towards capitalising on fluid gigs. We're heading towards a white-collar expert economy, an expert gig economy.

Businesses that expect a lifetime commitment from their employees – that want to permanently own their in-house talent – will find that eventually, the talent that they've spent so long hosting is going to leave them because the talent wants more than what they're being offered.

If someone has a permanent role in a business, then they're automatically disincentivised to do continuing professional development, and they're disincentivised to grow themselves. They're held back by their not moving with the times because they're happy, they're on a huge salary and they're not looking to change anything. These types of people are damaging to the business because they're not bringing anything new to the table.

Today, organisations have got a real opportunity to encourage *outside-in diversity*. This means allowing their talent to have multiple interests. Outside-in diversity is about enabling top talent to take on a trusteeship, to become a non-executive director, to take time off for a side hustle or to work on start-ups. The outcome of this will be that the talent is *less likely* to leave – firstly, because they've been given an outlet to pursue their interests, and secondly, because they're going to bring that diverse way of thinking back into the organisation. That is going to benefit everyone, influence how the business retains its competitiveness and creates a great place to work.

Most organisations that want to change and transform can't because they're plugged with legacy leadership skills and legacy knowledge worker skills. They're run by permanent people who have been there for five, ten, fifteen or twenty years who just don't know what they don't know. On the whole, the permanent executives are too busy to do extra training. They're stuck in business as usual, so over time they start to become irrelevant to the outside business world.

Future HR professionals and executives should start thinking creatively about the future of the business and allow people to have other interests and working opportunities. It's perfectly possible to encourage employees to pursue independent interests and then invite them back into the business to share what they've learned and invigorate the team.

Some businesses send people on sabbaticals or allow them time to pursue courses or degrees. There's no difference between this and enabling employees to go out and coach, mentor or consult, or to work on a side project. This sort of approach creates rewards for everyone.

In the industrial world, time is optimised. You must be at your desk between nine and five every day, you must be in a set location, you must work in a certain way – but why? The future of work is being decentralised because mobile technology and Internet access means that remote working will fast become the norm. New generations of workers will be able to find work regardless of how many times they move location.

Also consider the huge pool of talent out there. Parents and carers with young children, for example, predominantly women, are often locked out of the workplace because they can work limited hours or on a part-time basis. More and more, people are demanding work that fits around family life, and if employers don't facilitate this, they'll lose access to the talent and expertise that could be driving their business forwards.

Shifting from managing people in a time-based and an outcome-based way towards prioritising product-based outcomes and collaboration results in humans doing valuable work. It goes back to the human movement in the future of work – there's now a real opportunity for senior knowledge workers and executives to build something around what they absolutely love doing.

My story

I worked hard in the city for twenty years to get to a place that I thought I always wanted to be. And yet, once I got there, I felt completely unsatisfied for the first time in my career. It wasn't the perfect situation, it wasn't the perfect job – I wasn't happy, I wasn't healthy, I wasn't growing and I didn't feel as if I was being creative.

Looking back, I see that my work wasn't integrated with my life. I never achieved what Handy referred to as 'the balanced whole'.[11] I was miserable and unfulfilled despite having the status, money and lifestyle that I thought I wanted.

When you design your working life around what works for you, you stay healthy, both physically and mentally. I like to work in eight-to-ten-week sprints and then take time off. I like to have long weekends, side hustles and time for my friends, family and

---

11   C Handy, *The Empty Raincoat* (Cornerstone, 1994)

hobbies. I set aside time to be away from my business so that I can do other things that I feel are worthwhile and make my life meaningful. For example, I coach my sons' football teams and help out at the club. I work pro bono to help young entrepreneurs who are just starting out, and I'm on the board of an African youth development charity.

I haven't argued with my wife in two years because I'm not exhausted all the time and I have more time for our relationship. And I'm happier in myself, so I'm easier to be around. The life of working full-time as a COO wasn't sustainable, and when I finally took a stand and designed a life around me, everything in my life improved.

I'm just as busy now as I was then, but my life is so much more fulfilling because I'm doing the things I want to do. I've got a wide range of interests, and I'm not spending all my time with the same people. Doing the same things day in, day out, seeing the same people all the time, working within the same four walls every day – it can't be good for our mental health.[12] We all need breaks to keep us fresh, and we're now in an age where anyone can take a break from what's 'normal' and reinvent themselves if they want to.

---

12 'Mental health and substance use', World Health Organization, no date, www.who.int/teams/mental-health-and-substance-use/ mental-health-in-the-workplace

Five signs it's time to leave the permanent world

So how do you know if it's time for you to pack up that corporate lifestyle and move into the world of flexible work?

1. **You're done with the traditional ways of working.** The nine-to-five (or nine-to-nine), Monday-to-Friday job doesn't suit your lifestyle any more. You're fed up with having only twenty days of holiday, you don't like your boss, and the inflexibility of working permanently in an organisation means you're living for the weekend. You want to have more freedom and choose the work you want to do and when you do it.

2. **Your internal chatter is telling you to do it every day.** Your gut is telling you that going interim or portfolio is the right route for you. I meet people daily who want to break free from having a permanent job for the next ten years. They want something different and they know that flexible working is right for them, but they lack confidence or are unsure how to do it.

3. **People around you have taken the jump.** You've watched your friends and ex-colleagues go interim successfully. You know you've got the experience under your belt, so you're thinking that perhaps it's time to do the same.

4. **You've stopped learning.** When you stop learning, you become part of the problem. By striving for continuous improvement, you're challenging and disrupting the daily grind and harnessing and strengthening your skills while also working on your weaknesses. Are your skills today transferable to the next decade? If not, then a change is in order.

5. **You've built a brand.** You're sitting on a mountain of knowledge and have spent time creating an online profile to influence your reputation, finding your specialisms, setting up a vast network and maybe even setting up a financial safety net. You're already an interim worker to the world, so it's time you start convincing yourself that this is the right route.

Many people I talk to about this aren't financially sound or are scared of the commitment. My response is always the same – first and foremost, you need to mentally make the decision. If even one of these five signs applies to you, it's time to do something about it. Once you decide to start building towards your interim or portfolio career, the rest will follow. It's a marathon, not a sprint.

Something else to keep in mind: in the next three to five years, there will be portfolio and interim workers everywhere, meaning the market will get diluted. If you're going to make a change, get ahead of the curve and do it now.

Summary

- As technology evolves, humans are able to do what we do best – innovate, create value and build meaningful relationships.

- Seize the new opportunities to exploit in the new world of work, from flexible working hours and venue to a greater importance on personal fulfilment in the world of work.

- Retirement is a flawed concept and misses a huge opportunity to utilise experience and talent within organisations in a flexible manner.

- If you're not happy with your current way of working, it's time to make the change and to design a working life that continues to work for you.

In the next chapter, I'll discuss what to do once you've come to this realisation.

3
Be The Expert

Now that we've addressed what the future of work will look like, let's expand on that. Think about how changes in the workplace will impact your own ways of working, and consider how you can utilise your skills and experience to position yourself as an expert within the new economy.

What we can learn from children

Many frustrations come with the corporate way of working. Even innovative businesses with novel ideas and new approaches eventually lose their inspiration, creativity and drive – the corporate machine strangles it out of them. The bureaucracy, the excessive meetings, the highly pressurised environment and the fixed work hours leave no time for innovation and play.

We can learn a lot about how to live and work well by observing children. Above all else, children have freedom, which is what's lacking in the modern corporate world.

Think back to when you were a child. Do you remember how flexible your time was? How spontaneous you were? How many activities you took part in? My children have a portfolio of hobbies – karate, cubs, football – and their lives are crammed full of different experiences. One day, they might decide to be entrepreneurial and plan a cake sale or sell tickets to a youth disco. Other days, they'll attend parties, or visit educational places, or read, play a game or watch a film. There are endless opportunities and possibilities when you're a child and you're free to follow your interests. In fact, many children are pushed by those closest to them to actively pursue the things that most interest them. They're encouraged to explore and share the things that they're passionate about with others. They also socialise with different groups of people in different contexts regularly.

As a child, you also have self-interest – the desire to exclusively pursue your own interests and often an unwillingness to compromise or do as you're told. In many ways, children are more self-determined than adults. If someone tells them to do something that they don't want to do, they tend to make their feelings known. Their instinctive mentality is *I want to do this, and I'm going to do it*. Children have dreams as well as the self-belief and confidence to pursue them.

Once you enter the world of work, often all this changes. You lose your childhood outlook and your self-determinism. What you really want from life gets put on hold, and although you might still have dreams, you don't believe in them as much as you used to. You get a job, you get life insurance, you get a mortgage, you have children, you have your twenty days of holiday a year, and you start to sacrifice your hobbies and interests for those of your children. You wait until you retire or until your kids are older to do what you really want to do. You put freedom on hold and stop believing in the idea that you can design your life.

This can't be the right approach. We need to stop and think about the way we're living our lives and what we're teaching our children. Surely we have a duty to show them that adult life can be exciting too? If your children see you gaining just as much excitement from your life as they do from theirs, they'll receive a powerful positive message about what their own future could be like.

Applying a childhood mindset to the world of work

We're heading into a future where individuals are beginning to realise that they have a responsibility, both to society and to themselves, to create a place of work that people love being in.

Wouldn't it be wonderful if when you went into work you felt like a child again? Imagine:

- Having a variety of projects to work on
- Doing work that's outcome-based rather than time-based
- Engaging in social projects through work because there's a social responsibility at their core
- Taking holidays when you need them
- Going on sabbatical every now and again

It's just as important for adults to have variety, adventure and opportunity in their lives as it is for children. Let's look at what the children in our life have and do right now and use that as a starting point for the type of life we want to create for ourselves. For me, the future of work is about people loving what they're doing and practising work-life integration.

The Interim Revolution

With my first book, *The Interim Revolution*, I wanted to use a new business model and different methods to help businesses transform. I still wholeheartedly believe in the ideas that I wrote about then. *The Interim Revolution* is about bringing your value and the experience that you've gained over the past five, ten, fifteen, twenty or thirty years in your industry and selling that expertise to other businesses. It's about making the step to becoming an independent expert, which in the UK and Europe is called 'interim management' (I think the phrase is a little outdated now).

In my previous life working as a recruiter, I was at the cutting edge of the marketspace, which allowed me to see clearly just how many executives and senior knowledge workers were turning their backs on the corporate way of working. I saw an opportunity to create a brand-new consulting model – crowd-source problems to teams of experts and land those experts around outcomes. *The Interim Revolution* sets out a way to change businesses globally and presents the business world with an opportunity to transform by harnessing the power of experts as a service approach. It brings to life the sharing, collaborative and knowledge economy, which will help organisations shift into a twenty-first century operating model and prepare for future work.

I have no doubt that big, long permanent drives slow your organisation down. Rip up the rule book and start again. The best talent is *independent*. The people who can help your business have *already left* the corporate world and are going it alone.

From 2013 to 2016, I coached people on how to become interim experts. Since then, I've been coaching people on how to become portfolio experts. When I speak to people who've left their permanent role, I can see they feel liberated, often for the first time in their career. Many have been under so much pressure from boards, shareholders, government and corporate bureaucracy. I can see the relief on their faces – suddenly they've got choices and opportunities, and they feel as if their destiny is back in their own hands.

'I've not had a single day of regret since switching from permanent executive roles to a portfolio career. I love the variety and constant context-switching that comes with portfolio life. The more organisations I am working with at any one time, the more I learn: this constantly refreshing, live insight into the challenges and opportunities of multiple companies means I am able to spot patterns and apply the experiences of one for the benefit of another. I feel very privileged to work with

so many great companies and I wouldn't change my career choice for the world."
— **Sarah Flannigan, Chair & Non-Executive Director**

The artisan effects

In the 1930s, the world was a very different place. There were only a handful of big, commercialised brands. Instead, there were companies which were part of a community and which offered a personalised, artisan experience. People would pop to the local bakery to buy bread and get a new piece of furniture from the woodworker down the road. The quality of the products and services was high, and the customer service matched it.

Fast forward fifty years. People turned their backs on local businesses, opting for the low cost and convenience which can be achieved only by bigger brands. As everything became more industrialised, these smaller, specialised companies scaled up or closed down, and the artisan movement was put on hold.

As a result, there began a 'race to the bottom' as quality was sacrificed. Businesses got complacent. The top-tier level of thinking took precedence, and the models that once helped these organisations to grow were no longer fit for purpose. When the world of hyperdisruption reared its head, an organisation could no longer survive simply by being established. It was time to step up or be left behind, meaning these organisations looked to business transformers, in the form of management consultancies, to offer a new perspective.

In the beginning, these business transformers were able to offer value by understanding the issues these organisations, the marketspace and consumers faced. But as they grew, the profit-over-purpose mindset polluted the change landscape, and they began to face the same issues that they were trying to help organisations resolve. This created a knock-on effect, and we began to witness the collapse of companies such as Blockbuster, Woolworths, Carillion and, more recently, Thomas Cook.

In the current market, businesses need to be inherently agile to compete. This means no more five-year strategy plans or outdated business models. Instead, there needs to be a laser focus on faster reactions and innovative thinking to create continuous change.

In response, we're starting to see a shift back to the artisan movement as businesses turn to smaller organisations which offer unique, fresh approaches. Big brands have less clout nowadays. Companies are looking for personalised service with a 'community-first-commerce-second' mindset. This means smaller businesses that deliver value and genuinely care about the outcome are starting to lead the way.

Employee and consumer views on artisan brands are no different. As people become more socially aware of where and how businesses operate, they're looking for brands which reflect their ideologies and values. People are willing to pay a higher price for premium and socially responsible products, and they want to work for smaller, purposeful companies where they feel they can contribute something meaningful.

The high-street shops are making a comeback because of the artisan effect. Similarly, in the business world, people are questioning why they should go to the giant companies only to get sold complex multimillion-pound playbooks that won't fit into their organisation. Surely it's better to access portfolio experts and get an independent view without the baggage of a big brand?

The artisan brands are disrupting larger businesses because they realise that attracting, retaining and then, when it's time, releasing the best talent is the optimum way to get value for money and guarantee tailored service.

Gig economy vs expert economy

The gig economy represents a trend where people are looking to make money on a gig-by-gig basis, rather than through one permanent job. The low end of the gig economy is platform based and commoditised, so it's easy to see how this mode of working could be exploitative. The talent is commoditised, and the work spurs a race to the bottom because it's transactional and there's wage pressure. This is what I see as the blue-collar gig economy, and it's a very different model to the white-collar gig economy that I'm talking about in this book.

The expert economy is a knowledge-based economy. It's the talent that's the differentiator. It's centred on skills, points of view, strategy – in other words, expertise. The skill gaps are large, so the talent controls the experience and there's lots of growth potential for the individual. The expert economy rewards people who are at the top of their game and who've chosen to use their expertise to deliver value to other people or an organisation.

In contrast to the gig economy, the expert economy is top end, with big fees. People go to the expert economy because they're looking to solve a capability gap, which can't be solved elsewhere. People are fed up with using management consultancies with big badges. They would much rather use experts. This is why my business, Sullivan & Stanley, exists – to exploit the opportunity presented by management consulting fatigue and match business problems and needs with a group of highly curated independent experts fused with our consultants who can help resolve these issues.

The artisan effect is making itself known in the expert economy. The high-end talent is there to use, and it's a win for both the individual and businesses. The individual gets to grow, choose what work they want to do and provide for their family while sharing their expertise around what they love doing, and the business gets exactly what it's paying for.

WHO ARE THE EXPERTS IN THE EXPERT ECONOMY?

The experts I'm referring to are generally people in their thirties or forties and up to their eighties who went into the workforce or completed a graduate scheme and found themselves in the corporate world. They climbed the ladder and eventually became an expert in their field. After a number of years in a high-profile role, they got to the point where they recognised they'd become an expert in a niche area and could offer their expertise to other businesses for a day rate, or on a retainer basis.

There are experts to be found across all industries, and these individuals are able to advise, strategise and work with executives or a leadership team. They'll offer a point of view, hatch a plan and execute that plan or support others to do so.

> The expert economy is wide ranging, but invariably the experts that I'm talking about will have led a function, run a P&L, operated at board level or led divisions and their expertise is such that they can offer the sum of all their experiences.

Moving towards a balanced whole

People really like becoming independent experts. They really like the freedom and liberation that comes from remaining independent in a corporate, a business or a situation. Working in an advisory role means you can hold up the truth mirror, do some coaching, and influence and direct in a way that you never can in a permanent role.

It's a jump, but once the first anchor gig is behind them, and they've proved it generates a secure income, people can begin to visualise what a new future of work might look like. And not long after that, they begin to make changes that move their lives towards a balanced whole – in other words, they create a life around what they want to do and plan their work in a way that allows them to do it. It's about living the life they did as a child. I'll talk more about the balanced whole in the next chapter.

Healthy and happy centurions

Research tells us that there are several common denominators when it comes to longevity, and one of these is purpose. If you have a purpose, you're more likely to live longer and suffer fewer degenerative diseases than someone who doesn't.

I have a strong feeling that if my dad hadn't found purpose in his life after he retired, he wouldn't still be here. According to research on the Blue Zones, 'knowing why you wake up in the morning makes you healthier, happier, and adds up to seven extra years of life expectancy'. This research also reveals that the world's oldest people have 'close friends and strong social networks' and that being an active part of the community is also important for longevity.[13]

Portfolio working allows you to live with purpose for as long as you want to. There's no reason why you can't create multiple reasons to get out of bed in the morning. Portfolio working gives us a sense of purpose that enables us to seek adventure, excitement and flexibility and to build strong social bonds with different groups of people. As a portfolio worker, you can reinvent yourself as a child at play, while reaping the rewards of a longer, happier and more purposeful life.

---

13 D Buettner, '9 lessons from the world's Blue Zones on living a long, healthy life', World Economic Forum, 26 June 2017, www.weforum. org/agenda/2017/06/changing-the-way-america-eats-moves-and-connects-one-town-at-a-time

Summary

- The changes in the world of work offer us an opportunity to question what we want from our lives. Perhaps it's time to look to our children and their instinct for variety, adventure and creativity?

- Artisan brands are disrupting larger businesses. High-end bespoke talent is making itself known in the expert economy with its ability to present a unique and fresh solution.

- Portfolio working enables you to build a working life that combines freedom and autonomy with the potential for greater influence and an increased sense of purpose.

In the next chapter, I'll talk about how to move into a more balanced way of working.

4
The Portfolio Career

We've looked at how the artisan movement is re-emerging within the business world and how that presents us with opportunities to become portfolio workers. Now it's time to dive deeper into what it means to have a portfolio career.

The impact of COVID-19 on the future of work

COVID-19 accelerated the future of work in a matter of months, and I think it's fair to say that it changed the world of work forever. Traditional ways of working have been tipped upside down – working remotely is now normal. Thanks to the technology that we have access to, it's never been easier to become self-employed and work flexibly, and because of the global pandemic, everyone realises this, even those in more traditional, customer-facing roles. The pandemic has made employees aware that much of their work can be completed flexibly from home, and it's made employers understand that perhaps there are other (better?) ways to manage their businesses.

The pandemic has also raised the question of the cost-effectiveness of having thousands of people working in one location. How beneficial to the business is it to manage through a hierarchy? And how efficient is it to manage people in this way?

I've made all my big career moves after some sort of crisis, and I think that's true for a lot of people. A crisis forces us to stop and reflect on what we're doing, and I think COVID-19 was this kind of catalyst for many people.

I remember my wife homeschooling our sons downstairs with me upstairs running my business and leading an organisation which was, at the time, one-hundred-percent remote. Many executives were juggling a similar situation and wondering what life would be like for them once the crisis was over. Would they have a permanent role? And if so, did they really want to go back to the old ways of working?

Before COVID-19, there were senior executives who felt that they didn't spend enough time with their loved ones who then found themselves enjoying eating three meals as a family every day and being there for their children's bedtimes. People who had never worked from home regularly before found that they really liked it. The pandemic has led a lot of senior people to re-evaluate their ambitions and think about the way they want to work in the future.

The global crisis has catalysed the future of work in a way that nothing has before. Hopefully, we're looking at a future where work and life are more balanced.

The balanced whole

Charles Handy wrote about the balanced whole thirty years ago in his management classic *The Age of Unreason*. As discussed in Chapter 2, Handy coined the term 'balanced whole' to refer to a portfolio life made up of a range of activities. When these activities are considered together, they create a fulfilled life, a 'balanced whole', where all an individual's wants, needs and interests are fulfilled.[14]

Culturally, we're realising that we simply aren't wired to do one job forever. We're multifaceted creatures with multiple interests, and now, there are more

---

14   C Handy, *The Age of Unreason* (Cornerstone, 1995)

opportunities to monetise these interests. As we evolve and change over time, our workplaces will have to reflect this. We can see how much stronger the portfolio movement will become because of these adaptations.

What is a portfolio career?

Within a financial context, the word 'portfolio' refers to a collection of investments. You may have a number of investments on the go and track the health and wealth of these investments over time. Similarly, portfolio working involves having multiple 'investments' (interests) to manage and track – as opposed to a static corporate life where you have one investment.

Your portfolio of interests will reflect what you're interested in personally, satisfy your ambitions and result in a better way of life for you and your family. Put simply, a portfolio career is a working style in which you have several things on the go at once and multiple streams of income.

Who is a portfolio career for?

A portfolio career isn't for everyone. If you love your job and you're happy with the salary, a portfolio career is probably not for you. But if you're ambitious, want to pursue other interests and like flexibility and autonomy, you would be well-suited to a portfolio way of working. Portfolio careers are for people who have an entrepreneurial mindset and who have a fair amount of knowledge about their industry or niche. This way of working tends to suit executives over the age of thirty-five who usually, but not always, have interim experience and who are comfortable with change.

Great interims by their very nature already have a type of portfolio work arrangement because they don't want to be pigeonholed in a certain industry. They'll move from industry to industry learning, meeting people, encountering varied viewpoints and building their network. Switching to a fully portfolio way of working won't be too much of a shift for interim executives.

What does a portfolio career look like?

A portfolio career could be a mixture of regular employment, contract arrangements, consultancy work, coaching, pro-bono projects and work for charities and trusteeships. There's no set way to manage a portfolio career because everyone's will be different. Portfolio careers allow you to have multiple sources of income, to grow as an individual and to have time for passion projects, side hustles and family life. They're about total work-life integration.

The most successful portfolio careers are those where the individual has transitioned from a portfolio worker to a portfolio expert. They might coach and mentor resident directors, undertake core strategic work and, on the side, sing in a band, run a microbrewery, sit on the board of a charity or advise venture capitals on start-ups.

These five types of portfolio are those we see in the market (turn to Chapter 5 to learn more):

	The Lifestyler	A portfolio career with the flexibility to allow you to be in charge of your own time and live the lifestyle you want.
	The Side Hustler	A portfolio career that allows you to run your side hustle at the same time.
	Executive Portfolio	Before going 'fully portfolio', the individual runs a limited company and trades their own intellectual property.
	With Purpose	Portfolio activities are specifically chosen to sustain a sense of purpose.
	Portfolio Plus	Portfolio work is managed alongside a full-time, salaried executive role.

Design your executive life

I meet so many senior executives who are bored. Bored with their lives, bored with their jobs and bored with being a cog in a machine. And I can't tell you how many executives are completely dissatisfied with a sixty-to-eighty-hour week, being a shareholder and going round and round the corporate hamster wheel.

Over the years, it wears them down. Now that people are starting to vote with their feet, and it's accepted that you don't have to stick with the same job for your whole life, more and more senior executives are moving towards a portfolio way of working.

We all need to start living our 'good years' sooner. I've mentioned that the concept of retirement may well soon be retired, but make the choice to live well as soon as you can.

If you've got experience, expertise and knowledge, you can make yourself vital. You can create products and services around what you're great at and what you love doing – the things that naturally give you energy. It's time to design your life. You don't ever need to retire if you don't want to.

To design your executive life, you need to develop your portfolio thesis. What's going to work for you and how can it be designed? Are you going to take on additional client projects for more money? Are you going to spend time on things that bring you pleasure but don't necessarily earn you money? Are you motivated by cause? Do you want to get involved in trusteeships or become a non-executive director? Or maybe you want to reinvent yourself and become a global peak-performance coach?

You don't realise how much you know and how much your opinions are valued until you show up as an expert in a place where no one knows you. Previously, you might have been a CIO or an IT director but not that visible. You might have been seen only as the IT guy and been restricted in your ability to contribute to other areas of the business. But when you go into an organisation as an expert, everyone wants to speak to you. You're not just 'the IT guy' – you're the independent expert who's coming in to offer a perspective. You'll likely be asked all manner of business questions and have strong points of view on them. I promise it won't be long before you have your 'eureka!' moment and understand that you have more to offer than you ever realised.

But it's important to understand that the switch to portfolio working isn't going to happen overnight. It can take anywhere from three to five years to get to where you want to be, and as is the case when you invest in a financial portfolio, you probably won't see results straight away. You're taking a long-term view.

> 'The contentment and the better state of mind have made it so easy to do. Always surround yourself with people who share your vision, listen and have the courage to make the change.'
> — **Colleen Amos OBE, Co-founder of Amos Bursary**

Executive portfolio or portfolio plus?

Before deciding to move to a portfolio way of working, consider which pathway is most suitable for your specific set of circumstances and mindset. There are two ways in which you can achieve portfolio working – executive portfolio and portfolio plus. Let's look at each of them.

In an **executive portfolio** situation, the anchor gig becomes the catalyst for moving into a fully portfolio-based way of working. Before deciding to go 'fully portfolio', the individual runs a limited company and trades their own intellectual property. They realise the value that they can bring to businesses and want to own it themselves and make money from it.

They might be an IT executive, change manager, board executive or leader who's decided that the corporate dream isn't for them. So they get an anchor gig and receive a good day rate for their services. That day rate comes through the limited company they've set up, and suddenly they find that they're portfolio working.

The first anchor gig might be a six-month contract or a three-month rolling contract or four days a week on a fixed-term contract. Whatever it is, it gives them the confidence to leverage and build out their interests.

The anchor gig is usually based around the expertise they've accumulated over years as a senior knowledge worker and provides them with a steady stream of income. They then set up a limited company around their values and expertise.

In a **portfolio plus** situation, portfolio activities are managed alongside a full-time executive role. Often, executives use their full-time contract to develop their experience in related areas and build their sector knowledge. They then have a secure foundation for when they want to start generating other income streams.

Many people feel that self-employment won't suit them and don't fancy the idea of being their own boss. They don't want the pressure of having to find gigs, brand themselves and build their network, which is what a fully portfolio-based way of working demands. For some, having full-time employment plus the variety and flexibility of portfolio working is the best solution.

It's important to realise that at the moment, this type of working might be prohibited. We need forward-thinking business leaders to understand that top-talent people have multiple interests. This is evident in many smaller businesses now who allow staff extra days off to pursue voluntary positions, or encourage them to step into the limelight and share their thought leadership through articles, books, presentations and podcasts. It's important to realise that having portfolio gigs running alongside full-time employment isn't just beneficial for the individual – it's also of huge benefit to the organisation.

CASE STUDY – NICK POWELL

Nick Powell started his career as an IT program manager and then decided to become an interim manager. He began consulting for several different clients and picked up anchor gigs in which he'd work in an interim or senior executive role for several months to manage and deliver big IT programs for big companies. In the months that he was there, he'd build his network and list of contacts.

Nick enjoyed a healthy cash position via his limited company, so he started looking for ways to reinvent himself. He went on a course, wrote a book and became an accredited Bulletproof coach and a certified biohacker in accordance with Dave Asprey's world-leading Bulletproof coaching programme.

Now Nick runs his coaching and consultancy work in tandem, but he's also taken on a trusteeship and become a chairman of a mental health organisation. Also, he coaches his son's rugby team and runs a highly successful global podcast. He's getting income from his IT program management anchor expertise while continuing to reinvent himself as a peak-performance coach.

As a coach, he gets revenue from a regular stream of six to eight clients while having time to build his network and personal brand. He's growing his influence globally through his Paragon Podcast shows and his book. He spends one day a week marketing himself and doing speaking gigs. And all this came from an anchor gig in IT program management.

Is a portfolio career for you?

As mentioned, a portfolio career isn't for everyone. Many people enjoy their work or want to stick with a salaried position because of family commitments, external pressures and low-risk appetites, but there are ways to adopt a portfolio style of working alongside your main employment. I'll be talking about this in the next chapter.

Consider these statements.

1. You have more than one business interest.
2. You're ambitious and have a growth mindset.
3. You want to pursue a hobby but don't have the time.
4. You're not spending enough time with your family.
5. You like flexibility.
6. You're comfortable with change.

7. You like to be in control.

8. You're financially stable.

If more than five of these statements apply to you, then it's time for a change – you just have to decide whether you're going to go the executive portfolio or portfolio plus route.

Summary

- The past years have made clear that we live in a tumultuous world, and things aren't going to get any easier. It's time to safeguard your destiny just as you would your financial portfolio.

- Portfolio working reflects the realisation that we are multifaceted characters with multiple interests and experiences – multiple investments – to be monetised through a range of business activities and streams of income.

- You can work 'fully portfolio', in an 'executive portfolio' situation with an executive position as an anchor gig, or in a 'portfolio plus' combination of full-time executive role plus portfolio activities.

- Start thinking now about your interests and where your expertise lies. What are you looking for from your executive life and what is important for your 'balanced whole'?

In the next chapter, I'll introduce you to five different types of portfolio worker, so you can see what portfolio working looks like in practice.

5
Types Of Portfolio Worker

These five people have successfully moved to the portfolio ways of working discussed in the previous chapter. I hope that their stories might inspire you to do the same.

The lifestyle portfolio worker: Adrian Wakefield

'I took the plunge, and now I'm much better off.'

A couple of factors led me to make the change to a portfolio way of working. In my late forties, I reached a point where I looked at what I was doing and wondered if this was it. I wasn't sure whether I wanted to carry on as I was until I retired. This coincided with a change in leadership at the company I was working at – after a couple of months, it became clear that I wasn't entirely satisfied with the direction that the organisation was taking. I thought it was probably about time for someone with a different perspective and a different voice to come on board.

So I moved from wondering 'What's next?' to making a carefully managed exit. I had a lot of time for succession planning and to think about what I wanted for my future. Despite knowing that moving on was the right decision, it was still daunting – I was leaving a place of security where the financial rewards were high. I became quite introverted as I processed the change in my circumstances. Mentally, there was a lot to work through to prepare myself for the change.

I realised quickly that to find work, I was going to have to reach out to my network, so I took a diligent approach to contacting a lot of people I knew. I wrote to people asking them to recommend me, or refer me to their contacts, and I received a good response from that. I knew I also needed to create a profile and work on my personal brand. I did an awful lot of networking in the first eighteen months, and throughout that process I made it clear to everyone I spoke to that I was looking for three things: a recommendation, an introduction or an opportunity. I didn't mind which it ended up being, but having those three things in mind when networking made the exercise much more useful, and I wasted less time than if I hadn't had a goal.

The first piece of work I took on after leaving employment was a direct result of networking. It was interesting how open the guy was to working with me. I'd been referred to him by a mutual friend and because it was a strong personal referral, there was no hesitation when it came to bringing me on board. It just goes to show the power of networking.

I got a lot of value from the process of networking, and it led to good introspection. I had a lot of positive conversations, and that gave me confidence. I realised that there are many people who will help you if you give them the opportunity. Basically, you get back what you put in.

The one piece of advice I have for anyone who's thinking about doing what I've done is this: make sure that you're clear about what you want your next step to be and the sort of work that you want to do. There are so many different types of work available to portfolio workers – if you don't know what you want to do, networking isn't going to be helpful. Do you want to do advisory or consultative work, which tends to be more project orientated? Or do you want to do pure interim work, which means playing a real part in an organisation and helping to shape it? Or maybe you want to get involved in due diligence and advisory work? Or in helping and supporting institutions with technology selections?

In regards to portfolio working itself, it's important that you fully understand your financial outgoings, your commitments and what you need from the type of work that you want to do. There's a degree of uncertainty that comes with this kind of work, so you need to make sure that you're fiscally capable of withstanding the peaks and troughs.

You also need to be clear on what you want to achieve. Do you want to grow your portfolio work as a business? Or do you want to look after yourself personally? Do you want a lifestyle business? Or do you want to build an empire? When you're clear on what you want, it's much easier to create a business that fulfils you.

At the moment, I'm enjoying running a business that enables me to have the lifestyle I desire. I can take time off when I want to, sometimes considerable amounts of time, and I can fit in all the things that I want to do – and this makes me a happier and healthier person. Knowing that you're in control of your time and your life is a powerful feeling, and being accountable to yourself and knowing the impact that your choices have on your personal life is important. The energy you get from contracting directly with people and building relationships as part of who you are is hugely rewarding.

For me, it's about striking the right balance. Once I made the transition, I found portfolio working very rewarding. It won't suit everybody, though. Many will need more certainty in their lives than I have at the moment. For me, the uncertainty comes from not knowing how or when the next project will materialise, and what the work will be when it does. You need to be adaptable and flexible, and not everyone is like this.

But if you have the right mindset and can commit to a portfolio way of working, I believe that you'll reap the rewards of having a healthier work-life balance. I took the plunge, and now I'm much better off.

The side-hustle portfolio worker: Angie Main

'Being able to monetise something that you love is really valuable.'

My move to a portfolio way of working came about from a conversation that I had with myself when I turned forty. I started to think about the long term and saw that if I continued working in the way that I was, I was going to face burnout and collapse. I was worried about where I was going to be in ten years and wasn't sure that I wanted to stay where I was.

At the same time, I was irked about the consultancy I was dealing with at a large bank. They were charging a huge day rate, and I wasn't convinced that the quality of work being produced was worth the overhead. I had a lot of experience working with different consultants, and after a while, I thought, 'Hang on, I'm working longer hours than you, I'm working harder than you and I've probably got the ideas – why are you the ones making the money?' I felt like a cheap date, and I didn't like it.

The final straw was when I read a school notebook in which my son had written 'Mummy is somebody we see at the weekend.' That hurt and made me realise that if I wanted a relationship with my kids when they were teenagers, I needed to change things.

Knowing I had a wealth of skills and experience that would be useful to other businesses, I started looking for different opportunities. I was keen to move into a completely different industry, and because I've always been creative and happy with risk, I started to look at job swaps with product owners in Cadburys and Aston Martin. I even looked at the prison service for a while. I really started to think about my skills and values and the sort of work that would suit me and actually ended up working for Voluntary Service Overseas (VSO).

VSO was modelling a new proposition for senior leaders and executives in which they'd pair us with banks, universities and blue-chip organisations to find new opportunities for companies overseas, so I went off to East Africa for a number of months, where I worked with Barclays, SABMiller and a couple of research institutes. To my surprise, I quickly found that I enjoyed the work and was adding value. By the end of the placement, I'd written a PhD-length thesis on how VSO could capitalise on several opportunities. I was excited and realised that I was employable in different ways. That convinced me that I couldn't go back to what I was doing before.

Of course, before you make a change, you need to be sure that it's the right thing for you. When you've got the security of having been in an organisation for twenty years and you've got a mortgage and kids in school, you need to think carefully about what's the sensible thing to do. I found a good career coach and mentor, who helped me start thinking about myself more objectively.

I successfully applied for redundancy and used my period of gardening leave to do some pro-bono work. I also relocated to the north-east so I could be with my husband. I spent a couple of months working through what it was I wanted to offer to businesses and then began working as an internal consultant. I did a couple of projects for a previous employer and gradually started to find my feet.

I've been portfolio working for seven years now, and my life is filled with interim gigs that last about six to nine months on average. I've found that if you stay longer than that, you become like an old stain in the carpet – you're not really seen. You start contributing to the political stuff and suddenly you're no longer the outsider and your value goes down. At least that's my experience. Gigs of six months or so are perfect for me, as I like to be in and out quickly.

I've built up my coaching and consultancy work over the years and have also had time to pursue my side hustle, which is my craft ale bar. It's been going for two years. The ale bar was a way to give back to the community and do something with my husband. We wanted a project that we could work on together.

I also used some of my earnings from my new portfolio career to buy and renovate a cottage, which is eight doors down from the pub. The cottage has been taking holiday bookings for only a year, but I've already got a number of five-star reviews, which is really helping to drive things.

What I love about my life now is that I'm creating an environment for people. I've found that I really like serving people, whether that's in the bar or with the cottage. I also like to do a variety of things, and having a portfolio career has enabled me to do this. Having lots of different interests keeps me in better shape mentally, and I get a kick out of having various projects on the go at once.

I think about all the things I do like sliders on a graphic equaliser – I can push them up, I can pull them back, I can lean on different things. Essentially, I'm monetising my love of variety and creativity. I also give a percentage of the money I earn away. I set myself a goal every year to increase my giving. One way to feel good is to do good.

My advice for anyone thinking of going portfolio is, first of all, to find someone to be your coach, advisor or mentor – someone to chew the fat with. Turn your thoughts and emotions into something more objective. I think it's common for people, particularly when they hit middle age, to think, 'There's more to life.' Sometimes, you can make small changes that don't necessitate chucking the baby out with the bathwater. What is it that you're feeling dissatisfied about? What can you change? What's your gift? You might not have to go whole hog at first. It's worth taking a small step to see what else is out there.

If you're working in what you feel is a soulless organisation, create a network and do something outside of work. Carve out 5% of your time to do something pro bono. Do something that interests you. Really dig into and understand your strengths and values. Then, once you've decided to take the plunge, get some good financial advice and a good accountant. Make sure you understand the tax situation because portfolio working can lose its shine quickly when the money's not coming in.

Portfolio working isn't for everybody, but being able to monetise something that you love is really valuable.

The executive portfolio worker: Sarah Flannigan

'I've never been busier, and I've never been happier.'

Corporate life as an executive is great because you have a remit, a team and a thing to deliver, and you've got full accountability. And my life before going portfolio was all about that. I loved the sense that we were all working on something together.

The downside to that, of course, is that you've got to deal with all the other corporate stuff – filling out RAG reports (project status reports), going to risk and audit committees and attending a lot of training events, for example. I didn't think that I'd miss that part of corporate life, and I was right.

Before I made the shift to a portfolio way of working, I'd already toyed with the idea and had taken on two non-executive roles as a way of dipping my toe in the water. Both were rewarding trustee roles – one at Kew Gardens and one at the National Lottery Heritage Fund. So, in the two years before going fully portfolio, I was already experimenting and making myself busier. I discovered that these non-executive roles were an important source of spiritual and intellectual refreshment for me, which I hadn't anticipated at the time that I took them on.

I finally made the move to a fully portfolio way of working because I'd always wanted to be a consultant and knew that my approach would make me well suited to going into an organisation, helping them identify a problem, fixing that problem and then leaving. That's how I like to work. But I hadn't been able to make the move before because I'm a single parent and needed to support my family. I couldn't afford the risk of not having a permanent contract.

But then, in my last executive role, I was able to take voluntary redundancy, and that gave me the financial safety net to let go. I'd already taken the first steps by taking on the trustee roles, and in the first nine months after taking redundancy, I took on another three non-executive roles and some consultancy clients. In fact, I managed to achieve in nine months what I'd hoped to achieve in eighteen. Now, eighteen months after taking redundancy, I have seven non-executive roles and have grown my consultancy business.

All my non-executive roles came about as a result of networking except for one, which was advertised. I networked, went to various meetings and spent a lot of time talking to people. Not everything that I went for worked out, and I got a lot of no's, but I stayed resilient and kept going. Eventually, after throwing a lot of mud at the wall, some good-quality pieces stuck. It wasn't easy. I had to talk to a lot of people, pace the pavements and apply for numerous roles before I got to where I am now.

I wouldn't say that I'm a natural networker. I don't enjoy networking in and of itself. I don't like self-promotion or schmoozing, and I had to work hard to overcome that and force myself to have conversations with many people. But I didn't put pressure on myself – I networked with the aim of simply meeting interesting people.

I took the same approach to finding consultancy roles. I've got a number of clients now that I do a variety of work for, and they've all come through my networking efforts. Sometimes someone will get in touch out of the blue having remembered me from a conversation that we had years ago, and that will lead to great work. Other times I'll meet someone who I think is going to be a good contact and nothing comes of it. You never know which of your contacts will end up being helpful, which is why you have to keep networking.

What I discovered when I pushed myself out of my comfort zone was that there are loads of interesting people out there to have great conversations with. When you take the pressure out of the situation and resolve to enjoy it for what it is, great things can come of it.

Going portfolio is the best decision I've ever made. I'm happier and more fulfilled in my career than I ever thought I could be, and I speak as somebody who's always been happy and fulfilled in my career. I'm busy and the work is varied. The intellectual stimulation of going from one thing to another, of context switching, is something that I thrive on.

At forty-six, I'm relatively young to be doing portfolio work, and plenty of people advised me against it. I'm happy to say that they were wrong, but it is important to think ahead all the time. I've been out of my permanent role for only eighteen months, so I'm relevant and up-to-date as a practitioner. In five years that won't be the case if I stick to only non-executive roles. For this reason, I make sure that I keep up with the consultancy work where I'm properly rolling up my sleeves and delivering outcomes. This is even more important when you're working with technology businesses.

One other thing to note is that as a consultant technologist, you learn so much more than as a single CIO. I would have killed for the knowledge-share and experience that I'm getting now when I was a CIO, but there's really no other way of getting it. Now, I can be working at any one time across fifteen organisations that are all at different maturity levels and stages of growth, and it's amazing how the learning can be transferred from one to the other.

The more I'm involved with lots of different companies, the greater my knowledge becomes, and each of my clients gains from the knowledge I've gained from the others. And all the time I'm expanding my learning and experience. I love that.

I truly love my work now. I've never been busier, and I've never been happier.

A portfolio with a purpose: Colleen Amos

'The contentment and the better state of mind have made it so easy to do.'

Before turning to a portfolio way of working, I worked for The Learning Trust, which was a private not-for-profit organisation. So for me, portfolio working was a stepping-stone between the private sector and the public sector. Leaving the private sector and moving to The Learning Trust was a massive change for me. I had to leave behind all of the so-called perks and financial freedoms that you have in the private sector and make a lot of adjustments.

I left The Learning Trust when the ten-year contract that it had with the London Borough of Hackney came to an end. I'd been head of communications and marketing, and my job was to promote the change in education within the borough as it was taking place. Ultimately my goal was to build a community within the trust that shared a vision and values so that as an organisation, we could move forward together.

It was my dream job because I was able to combine my passion for education with communications and marketing, which is my specialism. Seeing the transition within the borough and being part of that was lifechanging, and I received so much satisfaction from doing that job. But it was hard work. We were trying to do something that was different and work in a way that was different than the council was used to seeing.

In 2009, after my parents died and while still working at the trust, I founded the Amos Bursary, which was set up to provide talented young people of African and Caribbean descent with the opportunity to excel in education – something that I cared passionately about. When I left The Learning Trust, I decided to use my time to help the bursary grow as a real initiative rather than as a hobby that my friends and I pursued.

My plan was to work for the bursary one or two days a week and also set up an independent consultancy, which would provide services to organisations, institutions and individuals because I believe in the importance of communications and the personal and professional development of individuals and organisations.

I'd trained as a coach and had done a lot of work coaching both junior and senior members of staff, and I felt it was a skill that I could take with me. I also believed in developing teams through communication, and I'd completed training in crucial conversations, another communications tool that I loved. In fact, without knowing it, I'd been preparing for my consultancy work the whole time I was at The Learning Trust.

When I started my consultancy, I had no idea what it would look like, but I knew that it would be my main source of income as at that point, the bursary couldn't sustain a salary for me. Because I'd taken early retirement, I had a financial backup of sorts, but in terms of setting up the consultancy, I hadn't got a clue what

I was doing. Fortunately, I'd upskilled myself sufficiently and gained a lot of experience in the thirty-odd years I'd spent in different private-sector companies I'd worked with, and that stood me in good stead to pick up projects initially. It was ultimately the coaching work that was the game changer – it was this experience that gave me the edge.

Then in 2012/13, the situation changed for the Amos Bursary: two major sponsors came on board. We were able to increase the number of students that we could help, and we started hoping that in the future, we could perhaps afford to pay salaries.

More corporates came on board in 2019, and with the Black Lives Matter movement and the focus on race and diversity in the workplace, the bursary's work has received more interest. As a result, we've had to restructure the bursary and bring on board more paid staff. We're no longer relying solely on volunteers. This means that we're now able to take the bursary to a new level.

The one piece of advice I would give anyone thinking of moving to a portfolio way of working is to make sure that you have some kind of financial cushion. As I say to the young men I talk to, 'Your passion remains your passion until it can pay the bills.' Also, don't rush, take your time and make sure that whatever you do, you do it extremely well. Surround yourself with people who share your vision, listen and have the courage to make the change.

When I left The Learning Trust, I had to downscale my life significantly but not to the point where I was going to lose my home. Because I knew that I could cover the basics and manage, I was able to really enjoy the journey that I was on with the bursary and my consultancy. The contentment and the better state of mind have made it so easy to do.

Portfolio plus: Bjarte Bogsnes

'I sometimes wake up and think that this is too good to be true.'

My switch to portfolio working came about not as part of any grand plan or scheme but because I started being invited to speak at company events back in 1996. There was a lot of external interest in what I was saying. In the beginning, the speaking engagements weren't much when compared to my usual job, but it's been steadily growing, and I now also facilitate in-house workshops for external organisations.

For the past ten years, the speaking work has been building and now it's roughly a fifty-fifty split between my salaried role at Equinor and my speaking work, and I'm extremely grateful to Mark, my employer, for letting me do this. I think he can see that there's a clear benefit to Equinor because we've developed a brand around this approach and are recognised for being forward-looking and active about thinking differently.

This approach is also starting to help us on the recruitment side – we're seen as an innovative company, and people want to work with us. There's also two-way learning taking place. I've been able to go into lots of different companies and speak to people honestly, which means I get to learn a lot and take those insights back to Equinor.

Working in this way is a win-win situation, and I'm really enjoying it. My personal credibility has also improved because people know that I don't have any hidden agenda and I'm not looking for sales because Equinor is financing it. I can't think of many people in a similar position, and I've found it a great place to be: partly on the inside and partly on the outside. The real beauty of it is that we keep developing our model and see it as a journey rather than as a project, so we learn to be braver in what we do.

I sometimes wake up and think that this is too good to be true. Now that I'm sixty-two, I could retire, but I'm happy with what I'm doing, so I don't see why I need to.

In terms of financial security, I'm still one-hundred-percent employed by Equinor; anything I'm learning goes to Equinor. For me, there's no financial risk in portfolio working, which can be a huge asset if you're at the stage of life where you have a young family or responsibilities that make it more difficult to make the jump. It's a balance that allows me to have my cake and eat it, an anchor permanent gig with my portfolio as a side angle and adaptable to my needs.

My advice to anyone thinking about moving to portfolio working is to think agile. Try it out. Start small. See if it works. If it doesn't, adjust it. If it does, keep on doing it. This isn't a marriage – it's something to experiment with. And again, because not that many are doing it, there's potential. Finally, don't underestimate the credibility that you're taking with you into your new roles. So many people don't have that because they're not able to work in this way.

Summary

- A portfolio career can be tailored for many stages of life, to suit a range of commitments and financial responsibilities.

- Start assembling your network and thinking about your interests and where your expertise lies. You can then begin to plan a portfolio way of working that works for you at whatever pace suits your requirements.

- Be clear on your next steps – what are your aims in terms of type of work, hours, location, and how you will find fulfilment?

In the next chapter, we'll look at what it means to self-disrupt.

6
It's Time To Self-Disrupt

Now that I've introduced you to some of the people in my network who are working in different types of highly successful portfolio careers, I'll ask you to think about what your portfolio career might look like and to consider the things you need to do now to achieve the lifestyle you want in the future.

The burning platform

In 2020, the world was presented with a burning platform in the form of a global pandemic. The speed of transformation that we experienced as a result of COVID-19 was unparalleled, yet perhaps not entirely unexpected. It had become clear well before the pandemic that the traditional ways of working weren't working any more, but COVID-19 created an urgent need as well as an opportunity for businesses to explore different models and move towards new ways of working.

Now there's more choice than ever, and if you're reading this book, you've already realised this and are starting to think about your next move. We can choose our futures and design our lives. Even if you enjoy being permanent and see your future inextricably linked with that of the company you're in, there's nothing stopping you from exploring portfolio options. You can still futureproof yourself by exploring side hustles, pursuing other areas of interest and investing in your personal development.

The old ways of working are dying out and the fourth industrial revolution is coming in. Business *must* change. Because if it doesn't, it will be an absolute disaster for the economy, the workers and, ultimately, the businesses themselves. We're in the midst of a work-related humanitarian crisis.

For every business that's content to carry on in the same way they have been for decades, there are plenty more who are looking to the future and putting their money, time and best efforts into digitally transforming themselves. There's no better time to look to the future and grab the opportunity to transform yourself too.

Businesses can do more with technology now than at any time in the past, and it continues to develop. Our current preferences revolve around, and are a product of, the digitised world, and we all need to either get with it or get out – there's no middle ground. This is why it's essential that you start to plan now for the life that you want to have in the next three to five years.

As I wrote this book, the UK was still in lockdown – the catalyst for me to plan my own portfolio future. The lockdown was my burning platform. I took the time to look at the things that I couldn't do any more, and to think about the things that I wanted to do more of. It opened up a multitude of possibilities to think about. I'm sure it was the same for you.

The time is right

Make the move now. Investing in your future today means that you'll reap the rewards later, but things don't happen overnight. Just as you put money into your pension pot each month to have a good quality of life in your retirement (if you choose to retire), you need to invest in yourself now to achieve your future goals.

I self-disrupted for the first time seven years ago, when I left the corporate world to launch a start-up. I did it again six years later, when I moved away from the recruitment industry completely. Now, I'm starting to think about it again and planning how to enjoy side hustles and more of my passions alongside my role at Sullivan & Stanley. COVID-19 has brought to life my growth mindset.

Daniel Priestley, one of my business mentors and the author of the best-selling *Key Person of Influence*, said, 'Your life today is the reality of the choices you made four or five years ago.'[15]

This quote resonates with me. It forces me to really look at the decisions I'm making now. What are you doing now that's going to help you to achieve the ends you want?

The biggest decision I've made, the decision that led me to where I am today, was to create a life that gave me freedom. I had a purpose, which was to change the game in business, to inspire the future of work and to create a consultancy business that could help me capitalise on that. But I didn't want to hand in my notice straight away, so I took time to consider my move, hang with the tension and make an informed decision.

---

15   D Priestley, *Key Person of Influence* (Rethink Press, 2014)

Six years ago, I put my time and energy into socialising with mentors, growing my network and getting my family on board with my ideas. It took me two years before I decided to jump, but when I did, I had a strategy, so there was less fear around the decision.

Now is the time to make the positive choices that will result in your becoming vital to this decade. You have to write your own story, lead your own life and build something around your own preferences – and the technology is there to help you do this.

The flip side of this great opportunity, of course, is that there's going to be a whole crowd of people trying to become portfolio workers. This is why you need to start planning, and defining, your personal brand *now*. Get ahead of the crowd.

> 'Pivoting to a portfolio career has been a journey, the first half building a network and confidence, the second half making intentional choices about the work I do and who I spend time with. It's always been about variety, making a contribution and growth. It takes resilience. Being self-employed keeps me on my toes but gives back joy, flexibility and the ability to take control of one's own energy, or even destiny.'
> — **Angie Main, people and culture expert**

Build the business plan

Changing your lifestyle significantly isn't just about shifting your mindset – it also takes self-discipline and new habits. You need a plan.

Research tells us that it can take many weeks to form a new behaviour.[16] Change doesn't happen overnight. But if you start to make even small changes now, you'll feel the benefits years down the line. It's important to remember that the move to a portfolio way of working should involve a three-to-five-year plan, and there has to be a long-term strategy underpinning the jump.

Every day counts. Set the scene for your future success. By doing things now that will set you up to take advantage of the times we're moving into, you'll be able to face an uncertain future with confidence. Why be beholden to an economic downturn and corporate politics? We know the corporate dream is dead, and we can use our skills and experience to reset how we work in a way that will futureproof us.

This will be an extremely polarising decade. If you can be replaced by AI, robotics or automation, or if you've got old-style leadership skills, you'll most likely get

---

16 P Lally, 'How are habits formed: Modelling habit formation in the real world', *European Journal of Social Psychology*, 40/6 (2010), 998–1009, https://onlinelibrary.wiley.com/doi/abs/10.1002/ejsp.674

disrupted by the new generation of workers. In effect, by *not* moving towards a portfolio way of working now, you're making yourself redundant. If you want to face the future with enthusiasm, you need to be change-ready – ready to self-disrupt. Set the wheels in motion now.

Get the support you need

When I decided to move to portfolio working, the first thing I did was find a coach, and I suggest you do the same. I found my first life coach based on a close friend's recommendation and received personal coaching over a period of six months. He worked with me to build out a plan and helped me tease out the details of what I really wanted in life. I realised, with his help, that I had nothing to lose, so I made the jump and started my journey with La Fosse back in 2010 where I learned how to build businesses.

Know that you're never alone. Change can be scary, but you don't have to face it by yourself. People are there to help you on your journey, and working with a coach will make the mindset shift a lot easier. I can hold up my hand and say without a shadow of a doubt that I'm 100% the product of coaching.

It can be difficult for senior knowledge workers and executives to reach out and ask for help – working at such a high level, you want to avoid being seen as vulnerable. People come to you when they have questions, and you're expected to have all the answers, so it can be quite a difficult thing to say, 'Look, I need some help.'

What I want to make clear is that it's OK. There's nothing wrong with leaning in and asking for help. If you sit down with a coach or mentor and say, 'I'd really like your help going over my portfolio – this is where I am and this is where I want to get to', they'll want to help you, and it becomes almost like therapy. They'll probably tell you what you already know, but hearing it from someone else gives you 'permission' to do it. Trust me, having this support in your life before making the big decision to jump makes everything easier and gives you both clarity and purpose.

You're going to be making the biggest move of your life. It doesn't make sense to do it on your own, and it doesn't make sense to do it without planning. I spent close to two years putting together a long-term strategy and getting my ducks in a row. You should do the same.

Portfolio working: A success story

In the last chapter, I introduced you to Bjarte Bogsnes, who developed a highly successful portfolio career without leaving his permanent role. I love his story.

While playing an active role as an executive in a Fortune 500 company, a business that turns over more than 130 billion USD a year, Bjarte has also written books, spoken at conferences, won numerous awards and delivered TED talks. The company he works for has encouraged and supported him to do these things because they're forward-thinking and appreciate the numerous benefits that this brings to them.

What Bjarte's example shows is that portfolio working doesn't mean that you necessarily have to leave your employment. You don't have to leave the permanent world if you don't want to. You can have multiple interests and gigs *alongside* your permanent role.

With work-life integration, people can have side hustles that end up adding value to the organisations that support them. This is the future of work. By raising your profile, you raise the profile of the organisation that you work for.

Even if Bjarte got fired tomorrow, he'd continue what he's doing. But the thing is, he won't get fired because he's adding so much value to the business. A business's best form of marketing is its people, and Bjarte's company recognises and celebrates this.

The great corporates realise that brand equity isn't as powerful as real people and real faces. Bjarte signals to the world that his company is pioneering business agility like no other, and the results speak for themselves.

In some ways Bjarte has become the face of the organisation he works for. I always encourage people who work for me to write a book or do a speaking event. When people are encouraged to stretch their wings, pursue their interests and develop their skills while in an employed role, the business will always benefit because employees will be happier, they'll be more loyal and they'll eventually become authentic, high-profile brand ambassadors.

Again, this is the future of work – real people representing brands in an authentic way rather than the power of a corporate badge.

Summary

- You know that things need to change, so why wait for the next burning platform? Look to the future and this opportunity to disrupt yourself and become vital to the future market.

- The best thing you can do for your future self is to think about your life goals now and take the steps to achieve them. Invest now for your future gains.

- It's important to have support on this journey. You're not alone – ask for the help that you need and take the time necessary to build a bulletproof plan.

In the next chapter, I'll help you make a plan and identify the steps you need to take to move to portfolio working.

7
Make The Jump

Now more than ever, you need to futureproof your-self to ensure that you remain vital in the years to come. I know it's not easy to leave a comfortable job and a familiar routine, but if you don't disrupt your-self, don't invest in yourself, don't explore the world outside your window, you're in real danger of becoming obsolete.

You can start preparing yourself to make the jump so that when it's time to do so, the fear is gone.

Money isn't everything

The first time I decided to make a switch, I was twenty-nine years old and living the corporate dream.

I was being paid a six-figure salary and was in a secure place within the organisation I worked for, but I was unhappy. I'd stopped growing as an individual. I'd been there for seven years, and I knew that I didn't want to be there for another seven. I didn't want to become institutionalised; I didn't want to hear the same jokes over and over and I didn't want to stay on the corporate merry-go-round.

When you're twenty-nine and getting paid well, it's tough to turn your back on what you know, but I realised money wasn't everything. I wanted my life to be about personal growth, learning, and creating something significant that had impact. The seven years I spent living the corporate dream taught me that I'm good at pulling stuff out of the ground and getting it working, making it profitable and building a management team around it. They also made me realise that I didn't get the same kind of energy from operationally turning the handle.

I looked hard at where I was and made a commitment to myself to change things. I knew I wanted to be tested in the upper echelons of business, have a world-class network, build a business, run a profit and loss, improve myself as a businessperson and get right out of my comfort zone. But how was I supposed to get from where I was to where I wanted to be? I was scared to make the jump because even though I was bored, I was also supercomfortable. What I needed was a safe way out – a bridge.

Switch-and-shift mentality

You know you're an expert in your field, and you also know that what you're currently doing isn't right for you. And deep down, you know that you can make it on your own. Despite this, switching and shifting isn't easy at all. When I made the switch, I had two young children (Sullivan was four and Stanley was two) and a big mortgage – equity handcuffs. I understand.

You need to start thinking of yourself as vital in a way that perhaps you haven't done before. This is the shift in mindset that needs to happen. You have to realise that you've got an opportunity to build something around yourself, around your core expertise. Understand firstly that you bring value to the world and secondly that you can make money from it. You can productise and then monetise yourself. You don't need an employer to pay you for your skills, your knowledge, your experience – you can sell these things yourself and be far, far happier.

Think about all the experience you've gained in the years you've been working at the level you have in your industry and then create a work-life integration centre around it. The aim of the game here is to make yourself so valuable, so vital, that over time you create multiple revenue streams and lifetime returns almost without effort, in the same way that you would with a balanced financial portfolio.

The rewards of portfolio working are tremendous and well worth the work, but I also understand the fear around making the transition from permanent to portfolio. As mentioned, it took me two years to make the jump. And in that time, I gradually got less and less engaged and more and more frustrated with what I was doing. I kept telling myself that things would get better but questioned whether I even had the right to try to move away from where I was. It wasn't until I started to look at my life through a child's lens that I thought, 'Of course I can have that! Why shouldn't I have that?'

Ultimately, it was a shift in mindset – the act of thinking about my life in a different way – that led me to start planning to change things. The mindset shift must happen before you can start planning. And if you're reading this book, you've likely already made that shift. That's going to make your eventual move much easier.

I knew that the first couple of years after the move would be painful, but I also knew that things *had* to change and that if I was going to do it, I needed to do it soon because in a few years it would be too late. The market would have moved on and my skills would be redundant. I wanted to ensure I was relevant forever. And I knew that if I made the move, in four or five years I'd be having the best time with my children and they would see my work as a source of inspiration rather than a source of stress and unhappiness.

Now that I've made the shift, I'm happier, less stressed out and truly living the life I want to be living. I know that when my sons need me to be there for them, I will be, both physically and emotionally, because I'm no longer tied up in the corporate world and shackled to an eighty-hour work week.

Face your fears

Once you've made the shift in mindset, it's time to face the fears that will inevitably arise. There are going to be fears about bench time and about where your opportunities will come from. You'll worry about your partner's concerns because of perceived financial insecurity and about market corrections and changes to your industry. Revisit the five signs in Chapter 2. If these are resonating, you can't *not* make the move, regardless of the fears. Because the really scary thing would be to stay where you are.

Something that affects many people, including me, is imposter syndrome. A lot of people are held back from getting their first gig and putting themselves out there because they don't think that they're up to it. You might find that every time you're about to do something uncomfortable, imposter syndrome will come along and put the fear of God into you.

So you've got the mortgage monkey on one shoulder telling you that you can't possibly make the move and you've got imposter syndrome on the other telling you that you're not up to it. The thing is, our brains are wired to guide us away from scenarios and situations that are seen as threatening. Your brain is trying to protect you. Feeling afraid and doubting yourself and your abilities – it's all part of the human condition.

The way to overcome your primate brain is simple: prepare! Just as you'd spend time planning a big speech, an important presentation or a big trip, you need to prep to the hilt to make sure that your transition plan is completed to the best of your ability.

You'll never get rid of imposter syndrome entirely, and you'll never dispel all your fears, but you can quieten them down and put them to bed if you make a plan and get into good habits. Once you make the switch and start receiving positive feedback and begin to succeed, and then thrive, in the new world of work that you've created, the imposter syndrome and all those fears that were holding you back will seem inconsequential. But you have to make the shift to realise that.

Find your accountability group

When it comes to any kind of lifestyle change, account-ability is crucial. This is why people who want to get into shape hire personal trainers. We need others to hold us accountable for the decisions we make and the actions we take.

When you're planning your career move, find a group of people who will hold you accountable in the same way that a personal trainer would. An accountability group –people who are invested in your success and happiness – will set you on the right track from day one.

Every person's accountability group will look dif-ferent, but I suggest including a close friend, maybe your partner too, and a mentor or a coach. Mostly, you want four to six people who are on the same journey as you so that you can support each other as you make changes. You'll all want to see each other succeed.

Become your own CEO

The best investment you can make is the investment in yourself. As executives and leaders, we tend to lose track of ourselves. We're leading organisations and leadership teams; we're reporting to shareholders and stakeholders; we're the ones on the hook for business results; we're sorting out problems in the business culture and between people; and we're dealing with corporate politics. And that's just for starters. This leaves little to no time for family, outside interests, physical exercise or mental growth.

But once you start to prioritise yourself, to put yourself first, it becomes so much easier to deal with everything else and start making the right decisions for you. You should be at the top of the list of things to sort out because you're the most important thing on it. You must become your own CEO. Just as the CEO of a company looks after the interests of the business with a view to growing it, you need to start looking after your own interests to grow yourself.

Build your personal boardroom

Once you've become your own CEO, build yourself a boardroom. If you want to grow, you'll need to have at least five people in your personal boardroom who will stay on this journey with you – people you can trust to help you make the right decisions and call you out when you make bad ones.

It doesn't matter who's in your boardroom as long as you trust their judgement and respect their opinions. The people in your boardroom should be those who care enough to help you ride the highs and lows and make sure you achieve your goals. Becoming a portfolio executive isn't easy, so it's important to have someone in your boardroom whom you can call on when times are tough and you need to offload.

The jump project

Once you've made the decision to jump, you need to think about what that first step looks like. Building a good network is key (I'll talk more about this in the next chapter). You also need to think about whether you're a consumer or a creator. If you're a permanent executive who's going around on the hamster wheel of budget cycles, shareholder pressures and corporate strategy, you're not in a position to create. You're a consumer. You might be online, but you're consuming other people's content. You might be going to events and networking, but again, you're consuming, not creating.

You're only as good as what Google or LinkedIn says about you, and the next generation of workers entering the boardroom knows this instinctively. If you can't be found online, you simply don't exist. COVID-19 showed us beyond all doubt that businesses and individuals are at risk of becoming redundant if they don't have an online presence. So as part of your jump project, you need to stop consuming other people's content and start creating your own. A strong online presence doesn't happen instantly. You need a lot of content and to publish regularly to gain traction and start making a name for yourself. Offering authentic insight will attract like-minded people into your network and magnetise opportunities.

You'll also need to think about your 'gig-able' skills and how you'll harness those in the expert economy. If the corporate machine has left you jaded, it can be difficult to identify your strengths and weaknesses. I suggest inviting three to five people that you trust and respect out to dinner and asking them to give you a 360-degree view on your expertise. This exercise is an important part of your jump project.

By doing this, you'll uncover your natural skills and discover passions, preferences and facets of your personality that you may have forgotten or overlooked. Once you understand what your natural skills are, and know where your true passions lie, you can start to build around those things.

A dinner like this can also help with imposter syndrome. You'll have people sat there with you – people you trust, respect and who genuinely care about you – who will tell you all the great things about yourself. Hearing people describe what you're good at will give you confidence and might even be the catalyst to make the jump. You might not realise just how much value you're sitting on until you do it.

Apply the same attitude to your jump project as you would to finding a new job. Think about the efforts you'd go to if you were looking for a new role. You might see headhunters, warm up your network, do a couple of speaking gigs, facilitate a round table or write a series of blogs. Raise your profile so that you become more and more visible to your network. This will help you make the jump without fear.

Let's go back to the idea of the personal boardroom. Each time I've made the jump, the people in my board-room have given me parachutes. They've advised me to take those steps to get into good habits and keep improving myself as an individual. I know I wouldn't have been able to make the big jump without those parachutes.

If you don't spend time building your boardroom and investing in yourself and you're suddenly made redundant and pushed off that cliff, you're going to have to find your parachutes after making the jump – now that's a scary thought.

'After a long corporate career in finance and human resources, I made the difficult decision to leave a great company and great colleagues to be able to devote myself full time to "Beyond Budgeting" at Bogsnes Advisory. I have seldom been busier or had more fun, choosing only work that makes me tick, and

feeling that more than ever I am making a positive difference to organisations and to people's work-life.'
— Bjarte Bogsnes, Beyond Budgeting expert

Your portfolio life

Your portfolio will be different from others' and personal to you because *you* are the product. You need to realise that your personal brand is unique. Once you do, you'll see that it's not difficult 'getting out there' because you already have the knowledge. You don't need to research anything, or spend time learning about your sector – you can leverage information you already know.

Your anchor gig will likely be linked to your permanent role. It might not be something that you're passionate about, but it will keep the wolf at the door, providing you with a revenue stream and a solid platform on which to grow your portfolio. The anchor gig should always be your big revenue stream.

Many of the people in my network who switched to a portfolio way of working have said that their anchor gig was something that they knew they could do and that felt comfortable. Think about the things you're doing in your present role. What functions can you perform with your eyes closed? What services could you provide to other businesses in your sector without having to undertake training or learn new skills?

Once you've identified those skills and raised your profile so your network knows you're out there, it's only a matter of time before you land your first anchor gig, and this will be your bridge to a fully portfolio way of working.

Summary

- Think about your investment portfolio and identify what makes you unique – your skills, passions, preferences and expertise. Building your personal brand and creating your own content will raise your profile.

- Remember that effective planning is key to facing your fears around taking this big step and adopt the mindset to embrace being firmly out of your comfort zone.

- Put yourself first and think of yourself as your own CEO. Building an accountability group and your own personal boardroom are part of your jump project.

Imagine how incredible it will be to build your personal brand around something that you love doing. Imagine how satisfying it will be to build a network that not only values your unique skills and expertise but also actively pursues ways of working with you.

In the next chapter, we'll look at the steps you can take to become a portfolio executive.

8

Becoming A Successful Portfolio Executive

You've made it to Chapter 8, so it's clear that you're interested in doing many different things, you're open to constantly reinventing yourself and you don't connect with your usual working pattern.

Here are the five steps I advise executives like you to take to have a career as a successful portfolio executive.

Step One: Adopt the right mindset

Everything in life begins with a decision, and the bigger the decision is, the more time you need to devote to executing it. Having the right mindset is crucial to being able to make the jump to a portfolio way of working.

It all starts by saying 'I'm up for this – I'm going to give myself the choice'. In doing so, you give yourself permission to develop new habits that will help you to become vital.

Step one is about making the decision and making the decision *now*. Of course it's going to feel daunting, but the key to overcoming these feelings of fear, as we know, is to be prepared and to have a plan. Once you've shifted your mindset and decided that you *are* going to do this, despite the fear, everything becomes so much easier. You simply have to put your plan into action. The dithering and the analysis paralysis are the biggest objects in the way of your success, and you're in control of these things – it's up to you to put them to bed.

The biggest mistake I see people making is not committing to a vision for their future life. They don't create their own burning platform. They know it makes sense to do so, but they procrastinate and ask too many people for their opinions. They don't admit that not having the safety of a revenue stream isn't for them. Many people tell me, 'Oh, I've got to go interim', 'Oh, I should get a portfolio', 'Oh, I should leave'. But they won't do any of these things because they haven't got the right mindset, the growth mindset, which you need to adopt to make the switch.

An important perspective

Before I made the jump, my dad said to me, 'It's obvious that you're not settled for the long term in this one permanent gig, but it's also important that you continue to give your all to your current employer. You've got a reputation to protect and values to uphold.' His words resonated. I realised that I'd be damaging my future chances if I screwed up my current employment.

You're only as good as your last gig. You need to go out into the world with your head held high and with a good reputation. Sure, I wasn't happy and I knew my employer wasn't right for me long-term, but I didn't want to compromise my integrity or fail to deliver what I said I was going to deliver.

His good advice continued: 'Deliver what you promised while also upskilling yourself. Make yourself vital, build your network and find out what you love to do and build a life around it.'

If you do this, you'll find that once you get to your horizon, you'll have a plan, you'll have money set aside and you'll have what everyone in the world craves, which is choices. This whole book is about giving yourself a choice – a choice to build a life around your preferences. But you *must* make the decision to change and then stand by this decision and make the changes *without* compromising your integrity or damaging your reputation in the short term.

Mindset is your plan, your choice, your freedom. Make that decision now.

Step Two: Network like a pro

How valuable is your network? When was the last time you did an audit of your LinkedIn network? Are you following up with the people you meet at networking events? How regularly do you network? Are you reaching out to people?

If it's true and you're the average of the five people you spend the most time with (according to Jim Rohn),[17] what does this mean for you? Who are the five people you hang around with most in the business world? If they're the same executives you've been working with for years and who use you as a sounding board to moan about the company you're working for, then maybe you need to switch things up? Find some new people to hang out with?

---

17   A Groth, 'You're the average of the five people you spend the most time with', Business Insider, 24 July 2012, www.businessinsider.com / jim-rohn-youre-the-average-of-the-five-people-you-spend-the-most-time-with-2012-7?r=US&IR=T

One of the things I did in the two years before I handed in my notice was build my network capital. In this decade, network capital is as important as your pension pot. You might use a financial planner to keep you accountable to drip feed cash into it; the interest will compound to give you a payback at some point. Do the same with your network capital.

In fact, if you're not building your network right now, you need to seriously rethink your approach.

EXERCISE – YOUR NETWORK SPIDER DIAGRAM

This is a quick exercise to enable you to map your network on LinkedIn. As the name suggests, you lay out your network to look a little like a spider. You are in the middle, warming up your network and reconnecting, with lines that branch out to add more connections you would like to re-kindle. This is best done over a strong coffee as you reach out and reconnect.

I once had a client who was reluctant to map out his network – he didn't see the point and said he didn't have the time. I asked him to do it just to humour me and he came back to me with the results. He told me that when he was working as an IT program manager, he knew a business analyst who was destined for great things. During an audit of his connections on LinkedIn, he noticed that this guy was now head of consulting for a top-end advisory firm. He reached

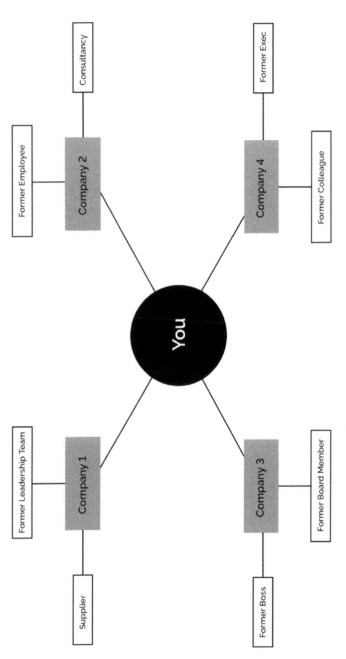

Example of your network spider web

out to him, they went for a coffee and three weeks later, he got his first gig. Now, this firm is feeding my client multiple gigs.

Often, your next gig is right under your nose. Do an audit of your LinkedIn connections this weekend. Spend a couple of hours on Saturday morning completing the exercise and see what it leads to. Your first portfolio gig might be right in front of you, but you won't know until you do the audit and follow up with some of your connections.

Step Three: Brand and position yourself

Ask yourself, 'Am I consuming or am I creating?'

What have you created recently? If you're so busy and burnt out that you're simply consuming rather than creating content that you're engaged in and passionate about, it's time to make a change.

In the not-too-distant future, most decision-makers will be millennials and people of the younger generations, so you have to be relevant in the digital world.

What do you love doing? What do you want to specialise in? What do you want to be known for? Start creating content around your answers to these questions, and this is what you'll become known for online.

CASE STUDY – CIO

A CIO I know started writing articles about the changing face of the CIO role and how technology is an accelerator for business transformation. Three weeks after he published this series of articles, IBM reached out and asked him to be a panel moderator. Then they asked him to speak at a key conference.

If you get found online, and by the right people, you can get access to all sorts of opportunities.

Step Four: Create your portfolio

It's important to know that at this step, there are no right or wrong answers – your portfolio career will be a pick-and-mix of your interests and specialisms.

In Chapter 5 I introduced you to several different portfolio workers. Now I want to introduce you to the different types of things that can make up your port-folio career. Of course, it's up to you which ideas you pursue.

A great way to broaden your horizons and take your career to the next level is to dip your toe in different waters. Some people take on not-for-profit, private or public engagements. Some become an advisory board member, a trustee or a non-executive director. They might do this work pro bono to get experience, but if they have the background, track record and experience, they could get paid for it.

These sorts of roles are good for networking and developing your experience, but they also allow you to give something back to the community, and to your network.

You might want to do what I'm doing and coach your children's sports teams, or sit on the board of a housing association or get involved in a church committee. It's about finding something you're passionate about and using that as a platform to start building your portfolio.

If people see on LinkedIn that you've got a permanent gig as a senior executive for X but that you're also a member of the advisory board for Y, a trustee at a charity, a public speaker, a mentor, etc, they'll see you as a portfolio expert and come to you with opportunities. It's time to start building your online identity and adding all these roles to your CV. No matter how small the side gig, celebrate it and start talking about it online.

Becoming a mentor is a big win. In Chapter 7 I talked about building your own boardroom. Well, this is something that you can do for others. There are so many mentoring programmes out there for start-ups, entrepreneurs and young professionals. There's always new talent looking to be mentored and guided.

You've built up years of experience – where can you use it? If you're in the right mindset, if you've made the decision to do this, you should now be appreciating the value you're sitting on and starting to think about how you can pass it on.

CASE STUDY – MARTIN MCPHEE

I needed someone on my board at Sullivan & Stanley to help me accelerate my business. I found Martin McPhee on LinkedIn. He was talking about stuff that I'm interested in and came across as having the sort of gravitas I needed.

He had multiple interests and experiences listed on his profile, and that showed me that he was the sort of person I wanted to talk to. I could see that he'd worked for the past three years running global consultant services for Cisco, that he was an advisory board member of an executive search firm, a member of the board of trustees for a charity, a board member for a real estate play in India and an operating partner for a private equity firm. He also ran a small consulting side gig around his own IP.

Looking at his profile, I thought, 'This is my guy!' I reached out to him cold and hired him, just like that. Now he sits on my board and he provided enormous value to the business during the pandemic.

Step Five: Form the habits

Once you've changed your mindset and you've started thinking about how to grow your portfolio, it's time to form the right habits. If you can get into the habit of doing the following five things now, in two or three months, these will be part of your normal way of working.

1. Save money – cancel unnecessary direct debits and cut down on the expensive holidays and luxury items.

2. Create content – provide solutions or a different perspective.

3. Develop yourself – build your portfolio, do a course, join an accountability group, etc.

4. Network – make time to meet new people and reconnect with old contacts.

5. Give back – help others by mentoring and coaching.

Summary

There are five steps to becoming a successful portfolio executive:

1. Get into the right mindset to make the decision and make it now.

2. Network, network, network – look at your LinkedIn and contacts and build your network capital.

3. Create rather than consume content – you need to be relevant in the digital world.

4. Build your portfolio with options that provide the personal and professional fulfilment you are looking to achieve.

5. Form good habits around developing yourself and your brand.

By now you should see that it really is possible to have the future you want. It's time to change your life.

In the next chapter, we'll dive into the Seven Switch Challenge.

9
Seven Switch Challenge

We've talked about the things that you need to do to set yourself up for a career as a successful portfolio executive. Now I'm going to show you exactly how to go about doing them.

This is the Seven Switch Challenge. Once you've completed these seven steps, you'll be on your way to living the life you want – one that will energise you. For each of these steps, there's a 'smartcut' that you can take to make the switch even easier.

One: Lean in and own it

You've made the mindset shift. The decision's been made and the hard part is done. Now you need to lean in and own the change.

This means start saving. What's your time frame? Are you going to stay in your permanent job for the time being and go with a longer-term portfolio strategy? Or is the game up now? Do you need to get out within six months? Twelve months? Regardless of your timeline, get your house in order, and this starts with your finances.

Start living as if you're in a recession. Take the willpower out of it and set up a direct debit into a savings account. Don't think about it – just do it, and do it now. You need to adopt a recession-spending mindset so that when you make the jump, you know you can support yourself and your family for six months.

You also have to know how financially stable you need to be to feel at ease. Not everyone can just drop one career and start another without any income to keep them sustained. Some people have savings and others have support from families and friends, but others have huge financial commitments. If you're going to give yourself a choice, make sure that your decision is financially viable.

There will be an element of sacrifice that comes with the jump. You'll sacrifice your time to build your network and write your content, and you'll sacrifice your quality of life in the short term. But remember, the process of making the switch will take only eighteen months to three years. In the wider scheme of things, this is nothing.

Use this time to reduce your debt and get into the mindset of saving for a rainy day because when you move to portfolio, your income will be variable. If you're under pressure to pay off a huge mortgage or service an expensive lifestyle, a fluctuating income could really stress you out.

When I decided to follow this process, I lived as if I were going through a recession, just as I did when I started my business. Every penny counted, and I set a tight budget. We stopped the expensive holidays and stayed with my parents for our summer holidays instead. We cancelled the Sky TV, stopped all the unnecessary direct debits and cut back on everything that wasn't absolutely essential. We did this so we could save enough money to cover my family and me for about six to nine months.

SMARTCUT

Cancel all unnecessary expenses and set up a direct debit into a savings account to cover yourself for 9 to 12 months while you begin your portfolio career.

Two: Hand-pick people to take to lunch

You're now an expert, and you're going to be creating a portfolio career around that expertise, so you need to get a 360-degree view of who you are and where your strengths lie.

Choose three to five people to take to lunch. They need to be people who've known you for a long time and know you well. Tell them that you've decided to build a career around what you do best and that you're toying with whether to go all in and become a portfolio expert or stay where you are and generate portfolio opportunities. What you're asking for are their insights and opinions regarding what makes you unique and what your strengths are.

SMARTCUT

Once you've got your friends round the table, ask them these questions.

- How would you describe me in five words?
- What value have I brought to you in my career?
- What is my unique ability?
- What am I brilliant at?
- How would you brand me?
- What would you pay me money to do?
- How should I market myself?

YOUR PERSONAL BOARDROOM

PARENT/GUARDIAN
DAD

This can be any parent or family member that is really influential in your life, that you turn to for advice for big personal and career decisions.

PARTNER/CLOSE FRIEND
HELEN

As they say, happy wife, happy life. But obviously, this can be be any partner or close friend - the one in your inner circle.

BUSINESS COACH
DAN

I'm a big believer in coaching to help me be the best I can be. Sometimes a coach can be just the ticket to break you through to the next performance level.

WHO DO YOU TRUST TO HELP YOU MAKE THE RIGHT DECISIONS AND SUPPORT YOU ON YOUR JOURNEY?

This is a peer who you work incredibly closely with during challenging times, who knows you inside and out and is close to your main specialism.

PEER TO PEER
KEVIN

I think it's very healthy to get different points of view from different demographics to challenge my biases and get me out of my comfort zone.

REVERSE MENTOR
CAL

As well as a business coach, I have a life coach who helps me to make sure I'm integrating life with work, as well as prioritising my mental and physical health.

LIFE COACH
WILLIAM

Three: Create your personal boardroom

You're now the CEO of your own life, so it's time to create your personal boardroom (see graphic). On your board, you want people who can guide, inspire and govern your switch and help you sustain it. Think about who can help you. Who's done this already? Who can coach you? You might want to include your partner, a parent, a life coach, a business coach, an old colleague or a former boss. And you definitely need someone who's already made the journey and working as a successful portfolio executive. Their experiences will be key in shaping your transition. You also need a good friend you can call when times are tough.

I change my personal boardroom every twelve months because I'm constantly evolving and need to keep things fresh.

SMARTCUT

Give names to the blank faces around the boardroom table. Below is an example of my own personal boardroom, but this could look different for everyone. You might have a wellness coach, a market maker – whatever suits you. Feel free to make it your own, but it's healthy to have 4–6 influencers in your personal boardroom.

Four: Go above the line

You need to establish yourself as a thought leader, so I'm going to challenge you to write five blogs about your area of expertise. You could write about your take on the industry, seven mistakes you see happen all the time, solutions to common problems or the future of X, to name a few.

Use your thought leadership and points of view, and start to contribute meaningfully to other people's content. Get active and build a brand around your personality. Write the way that you speak so that the people in your network get to know you.

You're sitting on an amazing amount of value. Now go and write about it.

SMARTCUT

When I started creating content, I'd go for a walk or run, speak my points of view into a voice recorder and have them transcribed later through Rev (www.rev. com). Then I shaped the text and published it. If you don't have time to shape it yourself, hire a freelance copywriter to do it for you. You can find some great people through the industry association ProCopywriters or use copy.ai as a content creation tool.

The chapter 'Seven Industry Mistakes' in *The Interim Revolution* came from a ninety-minute walk in the forest where I recorded my ideas in my phone – I then got the recording transcribed and shaped it. I later used that chapter as the basis for a series of blog posts and now it's a white paper.

Five: Reinvigorate and build your network

Do this as if your life depends on it.

I talked about the power of networking in Chapter 8. Now I want you to complete an exercise that will truly bring to light the great resource that your network is.

Grab a strong coffee, log into your LinkedIn account and do an audit of your current network. Map out your career – every position you've had, every project and program you've kicked off, everyone you've hired. Identify where you've exchanged value, which consultancies you've given work to, the coaches you've hired, the young hotshots who were working for you years ago – anyone you've lost contact with (see network spider web graphic in previous chapter).

If you want your portfolio career to evolve and remain interesting, you need a thriving network at the core of it. If you're curious about that network, then innovation, bright ideas, new revenue streams and magic will happen.

Make sure that you're meeting new people every week, tracking those relationships and finding ways to give back to your network so that it's reciprocal. This is what makes your network strong, and having a strong network means that when you make the jump to portfolio, you'll have a safety net to lessen the risk and reduce the fear.

When I was moving towards portfolio, I met three new people a week, and I had a system for tracking those relationships. Once I had a strong network, I started adding value to it and giving back. Being a good networker is about being a giver and not a taker. I've run a lot of networks and can spot a taker from a mile away – someone who turns up, asks for stuff, doesn't give anything back and abuses the network. Someone like this will take every opportunity to sell and leverage gain only for themselves. Don't do that. People like this have their card marked early on and don't last long.

Show up, add value, contribute and give back. When you give of yourself freely in your network, you'll reap the rewards.

A portfolio career can be quite lonely, and you might feel like a bit of an outsider at times. But if you can build a thriving network, you'll never feel lonely. Cultivating relationships will make you happier and have a positive impact on your portfolio career. Be curious about your new connections. Interesting projects and innovative ideas can pop out of conversations.

Once you've built up a network of contacts in which you're continuing to invest, put it to use. When you're making the jump, seek advice from people who are already doing portfolio work – learn about their journey; get into the nitty-gritty of its pros and cons. Further down the line, when you've established your portfolio career, you can pay it forward.

When executives are looking for work, they network intensely, with persistence and focus. They attend the wine-and-cheese evenings, the thought-leadership events, the speaker bureaus, the conferences, the webinars. They catch up with old colleagues. The list is endless.

Then, once they've landed a role, many of them drop their network. This is a big mistake. The winners in the world are the ones that treat the building, growing and cultivating of a network as one of their most important side hustles. You aren't just what you do – you're also a networker. You've got to network. If you're not networking, you're going into this with one hand tied behind your back.

There are plenty of ways to network, so go with your preferences. Some people like going to massive conferences and working the crowd. Other people prefer to join a tailored network that's run by a community leader.

Your network is your most valuable asset. I wouldn't be here today if I weren't continuing to grow, feed and cultivate my network. Yes, it can be time-consuming, but it's allowed me to make all the career moves and switches that I've needed to. My network looks after me because I look after my network. Remember: your network is your net worth.

SMARTCUT

Pay to play: if you don't have much of a network at the moment and can't afford the time to grow it organically, you can pay to build your contacts swiftly. Find a subscription networking group that you like the look of and sign up. You'll immediately inherit a network.

The money you pay to join will be well worth the opportunities it will generate for you.

Six: Tick two things off the portfolio checklist

Go back to the portfolio checklist that I introduced in the previous chapter:

- Step one – adopt the right mindset
- Step two – network like a pro

- Step three – brand and position yourself
- Step four – create your portfolio
- Step five – form the habits

Have a good look at it and choose two things on that list to tackle right now and decide on your next steps.

Seven: Commit to new habits

You've made the decision. You're going to invite people out for lunch, think about who you want in your boardroom, write content, start networking and find a trusteeship or an opportunity to mentor and coach others.

Now commit to these things for a minimum of twenty-one days. If you do this, you'll be well on your way to forming the new habits that will enable you to create the life you want to live.

SMARTCUT

Join my WhatsApp accountability group, where you'll meet people who are making the same journey. Contact accountability@sullivanstanley.com to join.

Summary

Take the Seven Switch Challenge:

1. Lean in and own your plan.

2. Hand-pick three to five people to take to lunch – ask for that 360-degree feedback in order to identify your unique strengths and skills.

3. Create your personal boardroom, your team to inspire, coach and support your jump project.

4. Go above the line – create those five blogs in your areas of expertise as the first part of your role as a thought leader.

5. Reinvigorate and build your network – communicate, contribute and add value in order to cultivate your team.

6. Tick two things off the portfolio checklist in Chapter 8 right now.

7. Commit to the new habits that facilitate your portfolio career – focus on building networks and relationships, creating your brand and finding the right portfolio opportunities.

Congratulations! You've decided to change your life for the better and go portfolio. Once you've completed the Seven Switch Challenge, you'll be well on your way to having the life you want in three to five years.

It's time to be your own pension.

In the next chapter, we'll look at the new frontier of work.

10
A Wider Perspective

You should now feel empowered to step into the new frontier of work with confidence. I'm not saying that your journey will be an easy one, but I can tell you from my own experience that the benefits of having a portfolio lifestyle will outweigh all the short-term sacrifices that you might have to make to achieve it.

Get the most out of the time that you're on Planet Earth. Adopting a portfolio lifestyle will give you transformational outcomes. Your work-life isn't a separate life – you have *one* life. Make sure that it's the life you want to be living and a life you live on your own terms.

In this final chapter, I'll ask you to consider the new frontier of work and what it might mean for you personally. If you take the steps I've set out in this book, there's no doubt that the new frontier will enhance your life rather than limit it. But remember, if you really want to change your life, you need to take the steps and start forming new habits now. The future is upon us.

The new frontier

It won't be long before people have multiple careers. We can see it happening already. Work-life integration will be non-negotiable for the next generations, and organisations of the future will be about leadership and coaching, services, knowledge work, and innovation and creativity.

Bloated organisations with hierarchies and layers of management and bureaucracy are going to see problems. This way of working isn't sustainable in the long term. It was dying before, but COVID-19 put the final nail in its coffin. Mark my words – this way of working will be gone by 2030.

Look at where you are now in the industrial world of work and think about where you want to be in the future of work. If you don't make yourself vital, if you're purely functional, you're going to be obsolete.

If you're vital you've got, or are developing, a unique skillset based around the things that you're brilliant at. People will pay good money for access to your expertise. If you're a senior knowledge worker or executive and earning a six-figure salary, it's clear you're working at a high level – you have experience, and people trust your judgement and your ability to get things done. It's not unrealistic to believe that other people will pay you similar amounts for sharing your expertise in a portfolio way.

'Two things above all others stand out for me in what I often refer to as "post executive life" – firstly there is something very liberating about the fact that what you represent, what you "sell", and what you bring to the table is quite simply you. No great big brand, no company line to tow, no one else's numbers to chase – just you and your accountability to your customer at that moment in time.

Secondly, it is the willingness to help and share – the countless number of amazing discussions I've someone found myself involved in these past six years – all fuelled by nothing more than being present, being curious and being open as to where a conversation may lead; and

all underpinned by the fact that "we never know when we may be able to help each other at some point in the future".'
— **Adrian Wakefield, CEO and Founder of Transforming IT**

Your new frontier

My new frontier looks like going on holiday when I want to go on holiday. It looks like designing my work patterns around what gets the best out of me. This isn't to say that I won't still work incredibly hard – it's just that I'll do it on my own terms.

I know that I haven't got it right just yet, but I do have that anchor. In three to five years, I'll be right where I want to be. And you can be too. There's a new frontier of work out there for me, and there's one for you too, but you're not going to be able to get there unless you take the steps to build that bridge over to it.

The world of work will be plural, and you need to be plural too. Companies are going to decentralise. The flexible workforce will be a big thing. Most organisations will likely start to regenerate their workforces every two to five years as opposed to every ten to twenty years so you need to continually invest in yourself and improve as an individual. Have a growth mindset. Stay healthy. Contribute to business, to the world and to others, your network. The world of work is going to be better for everyone. I have no doubt about that.

Give back

Remember that the balanced whole isn't just about your own life. It takes into account the impact that your life can have on others. Give back to the community; pay it forward.

You don't want to find yourself in the gutter with organisations that aren't based on a community-first-commerce-second ethos or don't have some sort of robust 'giving back' scheme; organisations that aren't purpose driven are going to be kicked to the kerb. But it's not just about organisations. Workers also must be purpose driven if they're going to thrive in the new frontier.

I've always built communities of experts, and when I connect them, wonderful stuff happens. In my previous permanent roles, I was usually the chief broker. I'd broker board problems with one set of people, and I'd broker the deal, the resourcing and the program to staff the resourcing. The work I do with Sullivan & Stanley is different in that it's a proper management consulting business, but it has the same ethos around community building.

It's lonely doing it on your own. It's lonely making that move from permanent to interim, permanent to portfolio, and it's fraught with risk, fear and sometimes failure. So giving, rather than taking, is crucial. If you give to your community and your network, those dangers are mitigated by others' support. Reciprocity is key to achieving the balanced whole, and also key to achieving success in the new frontier of business.

Do well by doing good. When you do good, people will remember you and recommend you.

The bigger game

Don't have a career and then a life. Have a life into which work is integrated. When you're portfolio, the many gigs, interactions and opportunities create a compound effect. Your network explodes, and you're futureproof for life. All you have to do to get a gig is pick up the phone.

The best person you can invest in is yourself. The difference between where I am now and where I was back then is incredible because I now look after myself first. I've designed something around me. I'm interested in everything that I do and I'm working to the best of my abilities in every aspect of my life.

I've got my business, my side hustles and my hobbies. I'm getting healthier, and I'm prioritising the things that balance me out. I'm more present. I'm a better husband and a better dad. I'm an all-round better person.

When you're working in a permanent role, you're always stressed out. Every executive knows this to be the case. You're building, delivering, leading – and unfortunately, your family doesn't always come first. It's just the way it is.

When you're living with the balanced whole in mind, you're calling the shots. You're the CEO of your own destiny. You're still working hard and you're still working full-time – it just doesn't feel like work in the same way.

Build a business around your life

Fishing is a passion of mine, and I stopped doing it for several years because of how all-encompassing things were with work and my family. Now, I'm starting to incorporate fishing back into my life, and I've drafted a plan to launch a business built around this: The Fishing Entrepreneur Network. With this new venture, I'll be combining my passions, my expertise and my network to create a community of business leaders and entrepreneurs who want to go on fishing retreats.

I'm now well into my journey to becoming portfolio, but it doesn't stop there. The next step for me is to build a business around my life rather than make my life about my business. I've already built a successful business that sustains me financially. Now, I can build a business around my passion, my hobby, so that my work will be integrated with my life in a way that it hasn't been before.

My future will still involve leading Sullivan & Stanley, but it will also involve monetising my passion to ensure that I continue to thrive and grow and feel fulfilled in the new frontier of work.

Here's the takeaway: once you've gone portfolio, you might want to look at ways to bring your hobbies into your business, or vice versa. Trust me, once you cross that bridge over to portfolio, you'll start seeing opportunities everywhere and you'll have the self-belief to take advantage of them and create something truly inspirational.

I hope by now you can see that the move to portfolio working is achievable. Hundreds and thousands of people have done it, and there will be tens of thousands, or millions, of people doing it in the next five to ten years. Get ahead of the curve and ride the wave of transformation. You know what you need to do, and you know how to do it.

I hope you feel inspired to take this first brave step.

Conclusion

There's a brand-new future of work out there for you. You don't have to work in the same way that you have been, and I hope I've proved to you that once you make the decision to change the way you work, to make yourself vital, actually making the change isn't that difficult.

Sure, there will be some short-term pain, and you'll need to sacrifice your time and cut back on some of your expenses initially, but the long-term gain will be well worth it.

I'm proof that once you shift your mindset and decide to make the switch to pursue a portfolio way of working, there's no limit to what you can achieve. You have an opportunity to be brave and create a road map for your future – this book is a resource to help you do that. I hope that the practical tasks and challenges help you on your way to achieving your balanced whole.

You know that this is the time to self-disrupt and that you have the experience, knowledge and resources to do it. There's so much opportunity in switching over to the portfolio way of approaching life. And you can't put a price on personal freedom.

I'm always encouraging people to reach out to me, and 75% of Sullivan & Stanley's consulting force is made up of former executives like you. I've coached hundreds of people who've made the switch, and I run six mastermind sessions a year on it. You're welcome to join us.

Sullivan & Stanley also has a community of people who are starting their journey to a portfolio lifestyle. If you want to join the group and create some accountability for yourself, get in touch and have a chat with me (www.sullivanstanley.com/contact). The Change Society and The CxO Society are our two main associate networks. By joining these, you'll immediately connect with people who've been through what you want to go through. You can access thought leadership and free training. We don't charge for this because we live by our values – it's important to give back to your network and the community that supports you.

Best of luck, make the decision and lean in.

It's time to self-disrupt, before the future disrupts you.

Acknowledgements

Creating Sullivan & Stanley to inspire a future of work for my children's generation wouldn't have been possible without my wife, Helen Lynes, supporting me every day since we met nearly 25 years ago. You are one in a million.

I also dedicate this book to all those brave executives who have made the jump to interim, independent and portfolio ways of working. You are leading life on your terms, making your own rules and owning it.

You are the brave ones, the disrupted executives contributing to a better world of work, advising businesses and people to be better.